CRITICAL ACCLAIM FOR
SO MANY THINGS TO BURY

"There's not anything good about Al Heidorns's life. Falling apart at the seams, Al's just not boy scout material. Heidorn has no where to go but six feet under. Chris Orlet's story is filled with top-notch witty prose and humor until the reality of Heidorn's choices leaves no one laughing. High fives for Orlet, a worthy author, who makes it clear some people continually make bad decisions."
—Wil A. Emerson, bestselling short story author

SO MANY THINGS TO BURY

BOOKS BY CHRIS ORLET

In the Pines
A Taste of Shotgun
So Many Things To Bury

CHRIS ORLET

SO MANY THINGS TO BURY

Copyright © 2023 by Chris Orlet

All rights reserved. No part of the book may be reproduced in any form or by any electronic or mechanical means, including information storage and retrieval systems, without permission in writing from the publisher, except by a reviewer who may quote brief passages in a review.

Down & Out Books
3959 Van Dyke Road, Suite 265
Lutz, FL 33558
DownAndOutBooks.com

The characters and events in this book are fictitious. Any similarity to real persons, living or dead, is coincidental and not intended by the author.

Cover design by Chris Orlet

ISBN: 1-64396-335-X
ISBN-13: 978-1-64396-335-8

*For Michele,
without whom there
would have been no books.*

"We just ought to wait a minute
before we decide to be so all-fired boy scoutish
and do the right thing. There's not any right thing."
—James Dickey, *Deliverance*

ONE

December 1979

IT WAS THOSE songs I used to hear over and over, the ones about Texas. It was because of them I ended up in this place. Six Lane Industrial Road, in unincorporated Denton County. It was there my engine, and my money, and you might say, my luck gave out.

There was not a single reason in the world for me to go to Texas, except I'd never been there, and I had this notion that it was a land of sunshine with lots of empty space to be left alone in. That and I'd always loved those country-western songs that talked about how wonderful it was down there.

"Texas is as close to heaven as I've been..."
"I saw miles and miles of Texas, gonna live there 'til I die..."
"Happiness is Lubbock, Texas, growing nearer and nearer..."
"Out in Luckenbach, Texas, ain't nobody feelin' no pain..."

People sure weren't writing songs like that about my home state. Nobody ever sang that Southern Illinois was as close to heaven as they've been—unless they were inmates in an insane asylum. But Texas now... that was where *Willie and Waylon and the boys* lived, and if it was good enough for them...

Besides, there was nothing left for me back home but bad

feelings and worse memories. What I needed was a fresh start. So, I crammed what few belongings I had into my '71 Ford station wagon and drove fourteen hours nonstop to the Lone Star State.

It was a mistake. I couldn't find a mechanic job down there to save my life. Just my luck, that we were in the midst of the worst economic slump since the Great Depression. Nobody—especially none of the garages—were hiring forty-seven-year-old white guys from up north. Not when they could have their pick of Mexicans for half the price. Not when the forty-seven-year-old white guy had all the hallmarks of a chronic juicehead: the red face, the yellow skin, the disheveled appearance, and a bad case of the shakes. Back then I was still fooling myself, thinking if I could only stay sober another couple months, Sandy would take me back. We could go back to being one big, unhappy family.

That's what I was telling myself, anyway.

Evenings were always the hardest. Sometimes, I'd swallow a handful of Sominex and hit the sack by eight o'clock, but that kind of living wasn't sustainable over the long haul. Two or three days were about all of that I could take. I even thought about giving Alcoholics Anonymous a try. A.A. had helped a lot of people I knew, but the whole Jesus thing turned me off. I'd lost what little faith I'd had in the killing fields of Korea and it wasn't coming back. I tried to picture myself squirming on a cheap folding chair in some dank church basement surrounded by sad old winos muttering empty prayers off a laminated card. It was just too goddamn depressing. I liked the idea of taking things "one day at a time," but the rest of it was superstitious mumbo jumbo, as far as I was concerned.

So, I tried to find other ways to distract myself from drinking, or thinking about drinking. I'd go for long, aimless walks in the evening. But as luck would have it, I lived in a part of town that teemed with bars and package stores, which was the only part of town I could afford, what with child support payments and my measly unemployment checks. I couldn't walk a hundred yards without bumping into a bar, and that was tough because there was nothing I liked better than bumping into bars.

Sometimes after work, I would drive to the city to this or that movie house. That year was a big one for pictures about outlaw truckers with citizen band radios. *Convoy. Every Which Way You Can. Highballin'. The Great Smokey Roadblock.* Then they went and raised ticket prices on me. I couldn't see paying $3 every evening to watch some fella driving round in a tractor trailer with an orange ape when I had a perfectly good black and white television set with a broken antenna at home that wouldn't cost me anything.

Home was a two-room efficiency in a noisy, cockroach-infested apartment complex out by the interstate. Two hundred a month it cost me. I don't remember too much from those days—thank God—except that sometimes in the stairwell I'd run into this emaciated old guy who lived across the hall. Occasionally, we'd stop and exchange a few words. I had a soft spot for the old coot. He had the air of a real dignified junky. Just the fact that he had survived for so long was impressive. It's a good feeling knowing there is someone even worse off than yourself. That gave me hope, I guess. Not a lot of hope, but a little.

One evening, I was in the parking lot pulling the plugs on my station wagon when the old man stopped by to bum a cigarette. I gave him a smoke and a pack of matches and he stood there studying the crumpled front end of the station wagon which I hadn't ever got around to repairing. We got to talking—or, I should say, he talked. He had a fine, mellow voice like Tennessee honey whiskey; I could have listened to him talk for hours. I could have listened to him read the phone book. Anyway, I learned how in a previous life he'd been a Baptist preacher in Silver City, New Mexico, and that he'd had a darling wife who'd succumbed to some rare and terrible blood disease, and after that, the bottom had dropped out for him. I've noticed that happens quite often to men of a certain age whose wives pass. Suddenly they're as lonely and disoriented as a little lost kid at the state fair. And they realize the only reason anyone ever visited on Thanksgiving or Christmas was on account of her, and that your grown kids can't stand being around you.

That's when he started in on the pharmaceuticals, graduating from prescription pills to heroin in the course of a few months.

Here the old fella paused and asked me if I'd ever tried smack. I said I hadn't. I wasn't even sure what smack was, but I didn't tell him that. He said he highly recommended it, said it felt like you was being hugged by Jesus, and no preacher or prayer or whiskey in the world could make you feel that good.

I don't know. Maybe he did feel that good, maybe he was happy with things the way they were, but objectively speaking—to an outsider, at least—his life was still shit, no matter how much the dope disguised it. Hadn't he lost everything on account of drugs—his home, his congregation, his faith? Everything but his crappy apartment and a TV set with lousy reception. I once asked him if he ever thought about getting clean, and he smiled and said nope, never. He was happy. He was doing precisely what he wanted to do.

I finished with the plugs, wiping my hands with an oily rag. We talked some more and, as evening came on, I found myself opening up to him. He was easy to talk to. I guess that was the former preacher in him. I told him I was trying to get straight, but damn if he didn't make addiction sound good. I told him how my wife and I had recently split up, and I nodded toward the massive dent in the front of the station wagon. I told him how the last straw came when I blacked out and drove through the front door of the house, and the damn thing nearly collapsed around me like a stack of playing cards. And how after that I went down to Texas because of some stupid country songs, and now I couldn't get a job and spent all my money on trucker monkey movies and sleeping pills. He suggested I give A.A. a try.

I told him I didn't really go in for that Jesusy stuff.

"Me neither," he said, then he bummed a cigarette for the road and said he'd talk at me later. I watched him shuffle off to the bus stop, no doubt going to buy dope somewhere. I was thinking to myself, that'll be me in a couple of years. If I make it that long.

Two

MY FIRST A.A. meeting would have been my last meeting, if not for this petite, thirty-something gal who was off by herself in the back row and who I caught stealing glances at me once or twice.

Her name was Jennifer, she said. Just Jennifer.

Just Jennifer and I chatted during smoke breaks, mostly meaningless small talk. I thought it strange that none of the other guys tried to chat her up. Maybe they were all married. Maybe they needed a woman like a hole in the head. Maybe they figured an A.A. meeting was a lousy place to meet women.

I went back a few days later, but Just Jennifer wasn't there. I went back again the next week, but she didn't show. In fact, I never saw her again. I asked around, but none of the regulars seemed to know or give a damn what happened to her. Probably fell off the wagon, one fella said. Or maybe she died or moved away.

Anyway, I suppose I had Just Jennifer to thank for getting me accustomed to A.A.. On my third night I was given a sponsor, an old recovering wino named Gus, who looked to be in his late seventies or early eighties, but was really only sixty-two. Old Gus had a knack for telling long, rambling stories that went nowhere, stories he told over and over, either forgetting that he'd already told them to me, or else not caring. I figured Gus was available to sponsor me because nobody else wanted him. It didn't really matter since I never called him, though I did continue to attend meetings.

I had just about run through the last of my savings when I lucked into a job laying carpet with a crew of Hondurans, or maybe they were Nicaraguans. The job made me long for my old auto repair gig. Talk about back-breaking work! I'd crawl around on the floor eight, nine hours a day then drive home, take a shower and head off to an A.A. meeting, then drive back to my apartment and soak my aching back in the rust-stained tub while I listened to the trash in the unit next door beat the hell out of each other or have loud, vicious sex or blast their shitty ranchero music, all the while trying like hell to resist the temptation to drink myself into oblivion or hang myself in the closet.

Put that in your stupid I love Texas song.

Once a week I'd call my two youngest kids—try to, anyway. Frank and Donna were both teenagers, so naturally, they were seldom home. Who could blame them? I was never home when I was their age—usually out running the streets, or hanging around on street corners, or smoking cigarettes on rooftops with other teenage reprobates. I hoped they had more sense than I had when I was their age, but I sincerely doubted it.

As for my oldest girl, she'd gotten hitched to a railroad man and moved some three hours up north. She refused to give me her address or her phone number.

Those nights, I usually ended up talking on the phone to my ex. I tried to tell Sandy about A.A., tell her I was serious about turning my life around, but all she ever wanted to talk about was the child support, which was always a couple of weeks late. Or else she'd give me hell for forgetting one of the kids' birthdays, or she'd inform me that one of them had been picked up for truancy or curfew or shoplifting or something. It was always something.

That Thanksgiving was particularly tough, it being our first holiday apart. I spent most of the afternoon dulling my brain with football and Marlboros, then at five o'clock, I called up the kids. Somehow, I managed to catch Frank at home. Right off the bat, he asked if he could come stay with me, which surprised the hell out of me. I figured he hated my guts for divorcing his mother and leaving town. Shows you what I know.

I wasn't sure what to tell the boy. I sat on the phone in my sad little kitchenette with dirty dishes piled everywhere and trash overflowing the waste basket and not an ounce of food in the house and I tried to imagine him staying with me—the way it was down there in Texas and the horrible mess I'd made of my life, and me going nuts trying to dry out and suffering through A.A. meetings most evenings. To say nothing of the constant pain in my lower back, the cramped quarters, the poverty, the nightly gunfire, the plagues of rats and roaches.

I couldn't see it happening.

"Did you ask your mother about this?"

"She said no."

I breathed a momentary sigh of relief. Then I felt the hackles on my neck rising. "What do you mean, she said no?"

"She said I couldn't leave in the middle of the school year. That it was too much of an eruption."

Eruption? "You mean disruption?"

"I guess so."

She was probably right. The boy had already been held back one year, and pulling him out now risked setting him back another year. He would be two years older than his classmates, and once that happened, he would drop out for sure. Like father, like son.

Even so, I was good and steamed. Sandy should have talked to me first. I was still the boy's father, goddammit, still head of the family, even if the family was as broken as a dropped egg.

I thought about allowing him to move in just to spite her.

"That's the best time to switch schools," I said. "Middle of the school year. Between quarters. Semesters. Whatever you call them."

"Could you come get me?"

"Ummm..." I tried to picture that—driving all the way up there for a big knockdown, drag out with his mother. I didn't have the stomach for it, especially not sober.

Maybe trying to spite Sandy wasn't such a good idea after all. I started backpedaling fast and furious.

"I don't know, buddy, maybe your mother's right. Maybe when school lets out... over the summer. I'll get you a bus ticket and you can come down, make you a little money laying carpet. They hire all them Hondurans, probably wouldn't kill them to hire a fourteen-year-old white kid."

"Fifteen."

"Really? Hell, you're almost old enough to drive yourself. Got your learning permit yet?"

"Yeah, but we ain't got no car, so I can't practice."

"Yeah, that sucks." I gazed out the ground-floor apartment windows. The glass was pockmarked with holes from a BB gun. They were the dirtiest windows I had ever tried looking through. Out behind the building, some Hispanic kids were burning an old sofa for Thanksgiving.

I changed the subject. "So, what's your sister up to tonight?"

"Beats me."

"What? She wasn't home for Thanksgiving dinner?"

"I dunno. I wasn't here."

"You weren't... neither of you were home for Thanksgiving?"

"I had dinner with the Lublinskis."

Jesus Christ on a cracker, what was going on there? The family wasn't even getting together for Thanksgiving dinner anymore. Hell, even the Manson Family got together for Thanksgiving dinner.

"What did your mother—"

"I got to go, dad. I only stopped in for a minute."

"Wait, where are you going?"

"I gotta go."

"Okay, but tell your sister to call me—"

The dial tone buzzed dully in my ear. I stood there in the

kitchenette, staring blankly at the receiver in my hand. Then I hung up and sat down in the lawn chair that served as my loveseat and put my feet up on the beer cooler that doubled as my coffee table and studied my cold, half-eaten Thanksgiving dinner of Totino's pizza rolls and a can of 7-Up. Outside a round of gunfire erupted. I was so used to it, I barely noticed. Same as the constant police sirens. I turned up the volume on the football game—Lions versus Bears—but it was no use. I couldn't stand it. The craving for a drink was too much. Anybody knows that it is physically impossible to watch football without a six-pack of beer. I switched off the TV and paced the apartment for a while, then I went through my wallet till I found a card with a phone number scrawled in pencil on it. I started to dial Gus' number; I was so desperate I was willing to listen to the old man's endless, repetitive stories. If nothing else, it ought to kill a couple hours. Might even put me to sleep. Then I remembered it was Thanksgiving night. The old fart deserved the night off.

As soon as I hung up, the phone rang. It startled me. My phone never rang, except for the occasional wrong number—usually a foreign sounding voice.

"Yeah?"

"Al? Frank said to call you."

For some reason, my daughter always called me by my first name. I mean, she would sometimes call me dad, but mostly it was Al. She did the same thing to her mother. She'd started doing it when she was two. I never understood why.

"Hey, honey," I said. "Happy Thanksgiving."

"Whatever," she said, which was about what I expected her to say.

"How was dinner?"

"Meh."

The flames of the sofa fire glowed through the thick living room curtains. God knows what kind of chemicals were getting pumped into the air, into those kids' lungs.

"Turkey and stuffing?"

Silence.

"Cranberries and pumpkin pie?"

More silence, then, "Russ was here."

I wasn't sure I'd heard right. "Say again?"

"Uncle Russ," she said. "He had dinner with us."

"Russ Cole?"

"Yes! How many Uncle Russes do I have?"

That made no sense. Why would my crotchety old cousin be invited to Thanksgiving dinner at our house?

I asked my daughter.

There was a pause. "You don't know?"

"Know *what*? What don't I know?"

"Mom and Uncle Russ are—you know—"

"No... I don't know!"

"They're... like... *going out*."

I felt the floor of my stomach fall out. I had to lean against the wall of the kitchenette for a second to steady myself. "What do you mean, *going out*?"

"Dating. Like, old people dating."

How was that even possible? Sandy was thirty-nine with three kids and an ass like the back end of a Buick, and Russ... well, he was a walking fart, a cranky old bastard with ragged teeth and bushy tufts of hair blooming from every hole in his body. He had to be twenty years older than Sandy. Sure, he had a few bucks, ran a successful septic tank cleaning business, but—he cleaned septic tanks, for God's sake. Maybe not personally. He hired some ex-cons to do that, but he used to, when he was starting out.

Then again, the more I thought about it, the more they seemed perfect for each other.

Still, divorce or no divorce, it felt like a double betrayal. My own cousin banging my own wife. I mean, there's certain things you don't do and somewhere on that list—pretty high up if you ask me—is you don't pork your cousin's newly divorced wife.

"How long has this been going on?"

"What? I don't know. A few weeks, I guess. He's *so* gross."

"A few weeks?"

"You know what he does for a living?"

"Of course, I know—"

"He pumps shit out of people's houses."

Normally I would have told her to watch her goddamn mouth, but with me missing in action the past couple of months—well, years, if you want to get technical—the days of discipline were long past. She was going to do what she was going to do.

"Well, not personally. He hires some ex-cons—"

"You can smell it on him! The whole house smells like shit!"

"That's your imagination." I tried to steer the conversation away from fecal matter and back to her mother's revolting romance. "When you say dating, what do you mean exactly?"

"Are you asking me if they're having sex? God, I hope that's not what you're asking me."

Angry female voices seeped in through my bedroom window. Sounded like girls cat-fighting in foreign tongues. I cupped my hand over my ear to drown out the noise.

"Just tell me—does he spend the night at our house?"

"I *don't* know."

"How can you not know? Don't *you* spend the night at our house?"

"I don't think so, okay?"

That was something of a relief. Just the thought of that ugly sonofabitch banging my wife—my ex-wife—in my own bed… in my own house… got my blood up.

"Does she spend the night at his house?"

"Al," she said, her voice turning whiny. "I feel like a spy."

"You're not a spy. And so, what if you are? Don't I have a right to know what's going on in my own house?"

"You asked me about *his* house. And besides, you're in Texas."

"What's that got to do with anything?"

"If you want to know what's going on here, you should

move back home."

Did she want me to move back? It was hard to know. With women, everything they said meant something else. The trick was to figure out what—and I sucked at that.

I don't know, I thought, maybe it was time. I mean, everything seemed to be going to hell, with or without me. May as well be with me. I was thinking about my house, too. How a few weeks ago I'd been talking to my bargain basement lawyer, and I told him in no uncertain terms that the house was mine—and shall remain mine—till I dropped dead, and it passed to Frank. Sandy could have custody of the kids, she could have the station wagon, the TV, whatever child support she could wring out of my measly paychecks, she could have my left nut if she insisted, but she would get the house over my dead body.

THE OLD HEIDORN homestead had been in my family for generations. My grandfather had built it with his own two hands—which you could certainly tell. I'd describe it to you, but I wouldn't know where or how to begin. It had been built over two decades in fits and starts, whenever grandpa had the time and the money and the inclination and was sober enough to drive a nail. It was constructed in three sections, none of which had anything to do with any of the others. The 1920's front section, which consists of the kitchen, an open sleeping area and a bathroom, was the most traditional part of the house with its red and brown brick exterior. The Depression-era middle section, which also houses part of the kitchen and the master bedroom, has an exterior of plywood covered in cheap asphalt siding, while the rear third (a small sitting room and another bedroom), finally completed during World War II, has exterior walls of cement block covered in crumbling concrete. The front entrance—the one I drove the station wagon through—is non-traditional, too. Just inside the doorway is a landing that leads up some steps to the kitchen and down some steps to an unfinished basement.

And finally, off the back bedroom, there's a side entrance that looks out onto one of the alleys, but they boarded it up in the Sixties and the outside stairs are long gone. The whole thing is covered over with a leaky low slung roof.

I loved that old house. I loved how there wasn't another one like it in the whole world. My older sister Anna, however, was ashamed of it, embarrassed by all the broke-down cars and junk that littered the front and side yards. When boys would come pick her up for a first date—which, truth be told, wasn't all that often—she would have them meet her at a neighbor's house or down the street at the drugstore. I felt sad for her even then, but me? I never wanted to live anywhere else.

Eighteen years after my dad had the heart attack that finished him off, and all us kids were either grown or planted toes up in a South Pacific boneyard, ma decided she didn't need all that space with all its expense and upkeep, and she moved into a senior apartment. Since Anna was still ashamed to be seen anywhere near the house, and my brother had been killed in the war, I inherited the property by default.

The day after I spoke to my dime store lawyer, he rang me up again to say my wife had decided to sell the house and split the profits. However, the lawyer said, she also knew what the house meant to me, so she was willing to settle for twenty grand in cash. Of course she was, the bitch. The whole property wasn't worth twenty grand, and she knew it. My lawyer said he had tried to talk her down, but that was her final offer. He said most folks in my situation would look at refinancing the home and try to pull out enough equity during the refi to buy out my ex, though with me earning minimum wage and not having any credit to speak of I likely wouldn't qualify for refinancing. I told him he didn't know the half of it. I told him I'd lost the carpet job the week before.

There was a heavy sigh on the other end of the line. "Looks like I'll be working *pro bono* again."

"Don't worry, I'll pay you," I told the goddamn vulture.

"Soon as my ship comes in."

"No offense, Al, but that ship sank a long time ago. It's at the bottom of the ocean with the *Maine* and the *Lusitania*."

I guess those were some boats I was supposed to know something about.

By now, things were beginning to settle down outside. The sofa had been reduced to a smoldering toxic ash heap, and the child arsonists had evidently grown bored and wandered off looking for a dining room set to torch. Across town, church bells tolled solemnly. They seemed out of place, ringing across that industrial-commercial wasteland, like rock and roll music in the cemetery.

"I'm sorry. What were you saying?" I asked my daughter.

"I said, if you want to know what's going on around here, you ought to come back home."

Oh yeah.

Maybe it was time to change the subject; I asked how her brother was doing. She had no idea.

"He's hardly ever home. He doesn't like Russ. I don't like Russ either, but Frank really hates him. They fight like dogs and cats. One time, Russ punched Frank really hard, and Mom didn't even say anything."

I felt the hair stand up on the back of my neck. The rat bastard. Nobody hits my kids, but me... Punishes my kids, I mean.

"What do you mean, he's hardly home? Where does he sleep?"

"How would I know?"

"You don't... Does your mother know?"

"Don't ask me. Ask her."

"Oh, for God's sake."

"He might stay over at his friends' house. You know, the Lublinski twins."

"Lublinski."

"Al, maybe you ought to move back home, then I won't have to be your spy. You can follow Sandy and Frank around yourself."

I ignored her little smart-ass comment. "I can't believe your mother allows this. A sixteen-year-old living on the streets."

"He's fifteen... and what's she gonna do, lock him up in the basement? She already told him he has to stay home at night. He doesn't listen to her."

So there you had it. The whole goddamn family was falling apart, with maybe the lone exception of Rose, who had gotten the hell out the minute she graduated high school.

That reminded me of something. "Is Frank at least going to school?"

"How would I know?"

"Don't you see him there?"

"Al, I'm still in middle school."

"That's right. I knew that."

I honestly thought she was older than that. They say girls are growing up faster these days, getting their periods sooner. That's what they say, anyway. She sure sounded grown up on the phone. When she wasn't whining like a little bitch.

"I gotta go, Dad."

Now I was "Dad."

The line went dead. I stared out the window for a while at the charred remains of a sofa sleeper, wondering if maybe I *should* move back home. I sure as hell wasn't accomplishing anything down here. I slipped on my work jacket and headed for the door. Maybe I'd take that walk after all.

THREE

I GOT BACK IN TOWN the Tuesday before Christmas. In some ways it was like it was coming home from the Army in '53, the way I was seeing everything with fresh eyes, the way a stranger would see it, the way the houses and cars and shops and streets, even the people look different, poorer, shabbier, more forlorn. There was no denying this was a dying rust belt town whose best days were behind it. And even its best days hadn't been all that great.

All those colored lights and holiday decorations weren't fooling anyone.

That's how it felt driving through the old neighborhood. I was curious to see if Russ' pickup would be parked out front, and I was ready to make a big stink if it was.

Only it wasn't. The house was dark, and the yard looked uncharacteristically tidy. Gone was the familiar assortment of junk—the used auto parts and scattered lumber—that I'd carefully collected over the decades. The husk of the 1970 Volkswagen Beetle I'd won in a poker game three or four years ago and never got around to working on was missing in action. As I pulled into the drive, I noticed the Century 21 FOR SALE sign. Above it, a smaller sign read UNDER CONTRACT.

What the hell was going on? Last time I'd talked to the

kids—which couldn't have been more than four or five days ago—neither one said anything about Sandy putting the house on the market. My worse-than-useless lawyer had sent me a letter saying Sandy had got some family court judge to compel a sale of the property. I guess I thought if I spoke to her face to face, turned on the old Heidorn charm, I could still talk her out of it.

I sat behind the wheel fuming, cursing Sandy and Russ and Century 21 and family court judges everywhere. I wracked my brain trying to think of some way to stop the sale, some scheme to force the buyer to break the contract, short of threatening his or her life. But it was too late. I knew that. A contract is a contract is a contract.

I left the engine idling and got out and went up the sidewalk to the front door. From the knob hung one of those plastic realtor key boxes. I tried my key in the lock but it didn't work, so I pulled on the doorknob and twisted. I gave it a swift kick, but the knob held. That figured. The door and threshold were brand new; probably the only part of the house that wasn't broken down or falling apart.

I went around to the side of the house, keeping watch on my neighbor's windows. There were a lot of crazy old women living in our neighborhood, and I could feel their evil eyes on me from behind their kitchen curtains. They would have recognized my station wagon, but you can never tell what people will do, and the last thing I needed was to have to explain myself to a police officer.

I cupped my hands around my face and squinted through one of the kitchen windows. The kitchen and, farther back, the living room looked dark and deserted, save for a few cardboard boxes and crumpled up newspapers.

Where the hell was everyone?

I went around to the back of the house. The yard fell off a couple feet there, so I needed something to stand on to see into the back windows, but damn if somebody hadn't cleared the backyard of my junk too. I tried the far side of the house where the ground was level. I tried to jimmy open a window, but it was locked or swollen or painted shut. One window had a long crack in it that made me wonder when that had happened and how long it had been there? I gave the frame a few blows with my fist to loosen it up and then I gave the window another try. It was no use. It wouldn't budge. Then, I don't know, something snapped inside me, like a banjo string wound too tight for too long, and the glass exploded around my fist.

I withdrew my hand, slicing it worse on the way out. A pretty, ragged gash across the knuckles, the skin detached like the flap of a loose tent. Bleeding like a stuck pig. I picked a few small shards of glass out of my knuckles, went back to the station wagon, and turned on the overhead light and studied the wound. This was no amateur cut; it was deep and long and hurt like a slap in the face… with a brick. I probably could have used a couple dozen stitches, but I wasn't about to piss away a hundred bucks on an ER visit. I went through a duffel bag of old clothes I had in the back seat till I found a relatively clean sweat sock and put that over the cut and wrapped it up tight with some duct tape I had in the glove box.

Christ, man, you got to hold it together, I thought. The storm that made me put my fist through the window had blown past; all that remained was a kind of heavy weariness and the stinging pain in my hand.

I took one last look at the old homestead, then I backed the station wagon out of the driveway and drove on down the alley. I turned south on Main, just driving, keeping my hand elevated, and trying not to bleed all over my clothes and on my seats.

I was heading toward downtown. Flying on auto-pilot. I was tempted to find a phone booth and give my mother a call, see if she knew where my kids were, but I decided against it. I was in no mood for her sharp tongue. Besides, I had a pretty good idea she'd say. *"Why are you asking me? You're their father!"*

Besides, I was all done in after the fourteen-hour drive, and I needed to dress my wound before I bled out. I needed to find somewhere to crash, some place cheap and away from the taverns and package stores, if possible.

I had a vague recollection of an old motel on the outskirts of town, a 1950s motor court that had seen better days, the kind of place you drive by a thousand times but never really see, a dull, familiar feature on a neglected landscape. I had always assumed hookers and dope fiends patronized it, but tonight I wasn't feeling too particular.

I found the place—Shaw's Motel. The neon vacancy sign looked like it had been out of order since the Truman Administration. The courtyard was deserted—never a good sign—but I didn't much care. At least the place would be quiet. I parked in front of the office and gazed out at the little empty courtyard, wondering how it was I'd ended up here. I never expected to live in a mansion on the hill, but I sure never thought I'd end up living alone in some seedy, skid row motel. Though if I had had to guess which was more likely, I suppose I would've guessed the motel.

There was nobody at the front desk, so I clapped the tarnished handbell and waited, staring out the window at the courtyard, which somehow seemed even more desolate with my station wagon out there. A Christmas special, *The Grinch Who Stole Christmas,* played on an unseen television set. Boris Karloff's telltale voice. Some minutes passed, and I clapped the bell again. A side door creaked and a large, middle-aged woman lumbered into the office. The kind of woman who must have destroyed a lot of bathroom scales in her time.

"I heard you the first time," she said, sounding slightly out of breath. She leaned on a pair of wooden canes that she manipulated to get around. With an immense groan, she sunk onto a stool, very much like a piano lowered from a second-story window. She paused to get her breath, and I caught her staring at my duct-taped hand.

"Evening," I said. "How much for the week?"

"Forty-nine dollars plus tax." She studied my face for a

moment, then her eyes went to my ridiculous makeshift bandage. I knew what she was thinking. A nutcase. He can't afford bandages. How the hell's he going to afford fifty bucks for a room?

"In advance," she said.

"That's alright," I said.

She stared at me for a moment and pushed her glasses up the bridge of her big old nose and shoved the register across the counter. "Fill this out—and try not to get any blood on my register."

"I'll try," I said. I managed to scratch my name down without bloodying the page, then the motel lady picked up the register and studied my signature. "What is that? I can't read your chicken scratch."

"Heidorn. Al Heidorn."

"You ain't related to a Jack Heidorn?"

"Not that I know of. Why?"

"Fella by that name killed himself in Room 12, about thirteen, no, make that fourteen months ago. Blew his brains out all over the mattress and walls. Most disgusting thing I ever seen."

I set down the pen. "Sorry to hear that."

"Uh-huh," she said. "Well, Mr. Heidorn, there's no phones in the rooms. If you want to make a call, there's a phone booth at the Gulf station down the road."

"That's convenient."

I paid for the week and the motel lady handed me the room key—Number 12, of course—and then she laid out the ground rules. No cooking in the room, no parties, no card games, and no drugs. As I walked out the door, she called to me: "We run a nice, quiet place here."

"When the guests ain't shooting themselves," I said under my breath.

Number twelve was the last unit, farthest from the office. I parked the station wagon out front of Number 12 and carried my suitcase in. The room was about what I expected—brown shag carpet, lone queen-sized bed, nightstand, lamp with a torn shade, and an old dresser with buckling veneer. Dusty venetian blinds over the windows—fully a fourth of the slats were cracked. The bathroom's toilet, sink and shower all had a bad case of rust and the mirror over the sink had lost ninety percent of its luster. I tossed my suitcase on the bed, then I went out to the station wagon and hauled in my Army footlocker, which I still had from my little vacation in Korea.

When I was all settled in, I sat down on the edge of the bed and rested a while. Then I took stock. There it was—everything I had in the world. I'd left home in a huff and had only grabbed a few essentials—clothes, toolbox, six-pack of PBR from the fridge, my semi-automatic. I tried to make off with a photo album, but when I went down the basement for the toolbox, my wife had confiscated it. Along with all the albums. Probably spent that night going through the pages, cutting my face out of every snapshot.

I studied the room, the walls and carpeting, looking for bloodstains, I guess, but everything looked so old and filthy you couldn't tell what was blood, what was brains, and what was something even more disgusting. I went through my pockets and came up with forty-seven cents in change. I zipped up my jacket, turned up my collar, and hoofed it two blocks to the phone booth.

The night was cold and overcast, not a light in the sky. A heavy mist hung in the air, and yesterday's snow lay hard in ragged dirty mounds up and down Main Street left by city plows. Nobody had bothered to clear the sidewalk in this part of town, and I had to fight to keep my footing and damn near broke my neck more than once. I was still in my Texas clothes—a dark gray work jacket with a patch over the chest pocket that read "Merle" (who I assume was the jacket's original owner), a Dickies T-shirt, Levis, and western boots—and I was freezing my ass off. I squeezed inside the booth and paged through the mauled phone book that hung from a chain. Must have been a rash of telephone book thefts. The overhead light was burned out, so I fished out my lighter and looked up Russ' number. I wasn't sure he'd be listed—a mean old snake like Russ probably wouldn't want people bothering him at home—but I found his listing, dropped a coin in the slot, and dialed the number. I wasn't sure what I was going to say to him, but I was going to say something. Maybe start with, *Hey cousin, I heard you're nailing my wife...*

Something like that anyway.

It wasn't him that answered, though. It was a woman's voice.

"Who is this?" I said.

"Um, who's this?"

"Donna?"

"Al?"

"What are you doing there?"

"What?"

"What are you doing at Russ' house?"

"I'm staying here," my daughter said. "Jesus, Al, don't you even know where I live?"

"I... well..." A pickup rolled by playing loud, thumpy music, something with way too much bass. I closed the folding door. "I don't get it. Why are you living with Russ?"

"You think it was my idea?" she said. "I hate this place. I want to go home." She started making those horrible, guttural sounds girls make when they're about to sob uncontrollably.

Meanwhile, I was trying to wrap my mind around this new information. It didn't make sense. There were still too many missing pieces. "Are you telling me your mother just moved the whole family into Russ' house without asking me?"

"Why? What were you gonna do about it?"

"I—"

"Al, she sold our house!"

"I know."

My daughter had progressed from light weeping to full-on snot-choking sobs. I asked her not to cry, but that only seemed to make things worse.

"I begged her not to," she cried. "God, I hate this place. I hate Russ. He's so gross. I can't believe she wants to marry him."

Her words hit me like a bucket of ice water. "Wait—are you telling me your mother's gonna marry Russ?"

"God, I wish I were dead."

"Jesus H. Christ, we haven't even been divorced two months! What the hell's the rush?"

A recorded voice cut in on the line. "*Please deposit twenty-five cents for an additional three minutes...*"

I fumbled in my pockets for more change. Pennies, a couple nickels, a dime, no quarters. I was three cents short.

"Honey, we're about to get cut off. Look, I just got back in town—"

"You're in town?"

"Yeah, what do you say I meet you and Frank tomorrow? We can grab lunch somewhere."

"Tomorrow's a school day."

"*Please deposit twenty-five cents for an additional three minutes...*"

"Well, hell, after school then. I'll meet you out front at three o'clock, okay?"

The line went dead.

I slammed the receiver down and kicked open the sliding door. I went across the parking lot to the gas station. A handful of zombie-looking customers roamed the aisles looking for Cheetos and beef jerky or whatever the hell the walking dead eat. I stood at the counter until it was my turn, then I asked the young, moon-faced clerk if I could get change for the phone.

"We don't give out change. You gotta buy something."

I called him a punk under my breath, which I guess I shouldn't have. None of this was his fault. He didn't make the dumbass rules.

I looked for something to buy and my eyes locked on the rows of half-pint bottles up behind the counter. A bottle of Seagrams 7 was calling my name like a Bourbon Street hooker.

Why the hell not? I thought. Here I'd been denying myself all this time, trying to prove to my ex-wife that a man could change. And for what? So my slimeball cousin could make a hole in the welcome mat?

I was this close to saying "Half pint of Seagrams," when this sanctimonious little voice piped up in the back of my head: *If you feel you're about to backslide, don't wait—call your sponsor immediately.*

I could have gone either way. But for some reason, I turned to the clerk and said, "Where d'ya keep the Ace bandages?"

He nodded toward the back of the store. "First aisle."

I went over to the aisle, but if there were Ace bandages, they were hiding from me. I picked up a tin of Band-Aids, extra-large, a bottle of hydrogen peroxide and some aspirin, and got back in line. I handed the clerk a five, and told him I wanted my change in quarters, unless they had some kind of rule against that. Then I went back to the phone booth. I couldn't bring myself to call Donna back, so I opened the phone book to the Yellow Pages and looked up the number for A.A.. I talked to the guy who answered for a long time, till I'd used up my last coin. I told him I'd lost the reason I was trying to stay sober. He tried to convince me I needed to get sober for myself, not for others. Getting sober because your wife is threatening to leave you is a terrible reason to get sober, he said. A good reason is because you want to be happy, enjoy the little time we got on this earth. I listened, but the whole happiness angle wasn't doing it for me. It wasn't that I didn't want to be happy. I wanted to be happy and handsome and rich and respected and all that. Hell, I wanted to win the lottery, too. But I had much more realistic and modest ambitions. Like avoiding starvation and hypothermia. Making it through another night without shooting myself. I didn't tell him that, though. I'd already told him too much.

He said there was a meeting about to start, not ten blocks from where I was calling from. Why didn't I come over? Hell, he'd come pick me up.

Chris Orlet

He had the hook in me, and he was fighting like hell to land me. So, I stopped fighting him. I told him I'd be right over.

FOUR

A COUPLE DOZEN STUDENTS were hanging out by the school entrance, giddy with the freedom of three o'clock. I had no problem picking Donna out of the crowd. She was the one off by herself, wearing a shabby green coat with a hood, sitting on the steps, hugging her books to her chest and staring forlornly at the ground. Everyone else seemed to be part of a group, dicking around, laughing it up—everyone except my daughter. I felt sorry for her—and that pissed me off. I wanted to go over there and grab one or two of them kids, shake them till their teeth rattled, and say, "What the hell's wrong with my daughter, you little shit asses?"

That would probably not go over well.

I couldn't understand it. I hadn't been popular in school, but I'd always had plenty of friends. Semi-literate ne'er-do-wells, sure, but friends all the same.

I left the station wagon parked on the street and strode across the half acre of grass, past the long line of yellow buses that snaked around the front entrance belching black clouds of exhaust. Donna saw me coming, immediately got to her feet, and hurried across the lawn to meet me before I could embarrass her in front of a bunch of stuck-up teens who already had a low opinion of her.

"Hey sweetheart," I said. I went in for a hug, but she sidestepped me and kept moving. I turned back and gazed at the clusters of teens. "Where's your brother?"

"God, how many times do I have to tell you he's in high school?"

"That's right. I keep forgetting. You kids grow up so fast."

All that got me was a disgusted sigh. We strode back across the grass—my daughter keeping a good ten paces ahead of me—and eased into the station wagon. After a couple of embarrassing false starts on account of a low battery, I finally got the engine going, and we drove north on Main toward the high school. Donna leaned against the door, as far away from me as possible.

"You told Frank we were picking him up, right?"

She stared moodily out the window. "I haven't talked to him."

"You mean you forgot?"

"I didn't forget. He didn't come home last night."

We were stopped at a red light. A police cruiser pulled up alongside us, and I glanced over at the young patrolman. He looked like a kid, not much older than Donna. Seventeen or eighteen, max. He must have felt my eyes on him, for he turned and gave me a cold look. Then the light changed.

"So, where was he last night?" I said.

"How should I know?"

I let the junior patrolman pull ahead of me, then carefully kept to the speed limit—a measly thirty miles per hour.

"When did you see him last?"

Donna shrugged. "I don't know, a couple days ago, I guess."

"So, there's no point going by the high school?"

She didn't answer. I waited till the patrol car was out of sight, then I made a quick U-turn. We drove in silence for a while till a Steak N Shake came into view and I pulled in there. The lot was crammed with long, old-people vehicles: Chrysler New Yorkers, Chevy Impalas, Ford Galaxies. We circled the restaurant three times, looking for a space. I'd just about exhausted my patience when this old couple exited the restaurant and shuffled over to their Buick. We sat there another five minutes, waiting for them to drag their crumbling bones into their car and back out and drive away. The time it took, you'd think they were piloting a 747 and waiting on take-off clearance from the tower.

I pulled into their space and shut off the engine. "Ever notice how old people have no concept of time?" I said. I felt awkward being alone with my daughter and was just trying to make conversation. "You'd think they have so little of it left that they wouldn't waste it like they do."

Donna turned away. "Why is everybody in our family so unhappy?"

"What? I'm not unhappy."

"You're not?"

"No. I would say I'm about… maybe a five on the happiness scale."

"Out of a hundred, maybe."

"Out of ten."

Even if I was unhappy, I wouldn't have told her. It's not something you tell your kids. You want your children to think you got your shit together. Of course, they knew only too well that I didn't have my shit together. Who can forget the way I blacked out and drove my car through the front of our house?

Among other things.

Donna opened her car door and hurried toward the restaurant ahead of me.

The Steak N Shake could have doubled for the dining room of a nursing home—full of grim, half-dead people. All it lacked was that heady aroma of urine, disinfectant, and decay. They showed us to a booth, one by the windows with a great view of the parking lot, and we sat down and stared at our menus in an awkward silence. A plain, middle-aged waitress brought us two glasses of water. The waitress studied my face for a moment, then said, "Al? Al Heidorn?"

I looked at her with a familiar sense of dread. Her face didn't register. Nothing. A total blank.

God, I hate it when that happens.

"Gwen!" she said. "Gwen Schwartz!"

"Oh," I said. Who the hell was Gwen Schwartz? Neither the face nor the name rang a single bell. Did I sit next to her in kindergarten or something?

"You don't remember me, do you?"

"Um. Sure. Gwen."

She laughed. At least I think it was a laugh. "We dated. In high school."

I smiled. "Of *course*. I remember. How are you?"

"That's okay. I wouldn't expect an *important* guy like you to remember me. Is this your daughter?"

"Uh-huh. Donna, meet Gwen."

"Hey," Donna said... barely.

"Hi sweetie." A long, slow moment ticked by. "I'll be right back for your orders," she said.

She walked off.

What the hell? You'd think I'd remember someone I dated. It's not like I had a lot of dates in high school.

Donna looked at me. "You dated her?"

I took a swallow of water and shrugged.

"You don't remember who you dated?"

I didn't feel like going into it, about my lousy memory and whether it was because of my drinking or because of the war or because who the hell cares?

"What'd she mean 'an important guy like you?'"

"I think she was being sarcastic."

"You think?"

"She was definitely being sarcastic."

I lit up a Marlboro and tried to think of some way to change the subject. "So, how's school going?"

Donna lifted her shoulders in a shrug. "Not terrible."

I nodded. Not terrible was good, wasn't it? I didn't ask about her grades. I had seldom asked about her grades in the past. It would only piss her off if I showed an interest now.

Donna stared at my hand. "What happened to you?"

There wasn't a note of concern in her voice, only vague curiosity. I studied the bandages. There were about eight of them and they were all about due for a changing. "Work accident," I said.

"Where do you work, in a shark tank?"

I grinned. That was a good one, but she wasn't smiling when she said it. She was staring out the window at the parking lot.

"So, do you know who's buying the house?" I said.

"I don't know. Why'd you let Sandy sell it?"

"I didn't. I mean, I tried to stop it…"

"So why didn't you?"

"She got a judge to go along with her. To force the sale."

"But I thought it was your family's house… your grandfather's house. It isn't her house."

"I know… It ain't right."

"Frank said it was gonna be his house someday."

"That's what we were thinking."

She took a breath. "Why him and not me?"

"I don't… Why, did you want it?"

"No. I was just wondering why he was gonna get it and not me. Just because he's got a penis and I don't?"

"That isn't why."

"*Why* then?"

"What's it matter? Neither of you's gonna get it now." There was an angry tug to my voice, and a few of the old farts glanced over at us. I stared angrily back at them.

"I don't care. I didn't want it, anyway."

There was a long silence, then she made a grab for my cigarettes, but I got to them first. I wagged my finger at her. "Uh-uh. Got to be eighteen to smoke."

"How old were you when you started?"

"Twelve, but I'm a bad example."

"Don't you mean a terrible example?"

"Yeah, well…" I frowned and looked around for Gwen

What's-her-name again. "Some service they got here."

Donna leaned her elbows on the table and rested her head in her hands. Her eyes rolled up to the ceiling. "So, where are you staying?"

"A motel, for now."

"Are you moving back?"

"I don't know… Should I?"

Donna gave a noncommittal grunt. "I don't know why you moved down there in the first place."

I took a drag off my cigarette. "Yeah, well… I guess I thought I might get my shit together if I went away."

"Did you?"

"Get my shit together?"

She nodded.

"Not really."

She looked away. "I didn't think so."

Gwen appeared at my elbow. She said she was sorry for taking so long, but they were short staffed. I told her it was fine, we weren't in a hurry, and Donna and I went back to studying our menus. I still couldn't place her. Not a single, solitary memory. I thought about asking her where we'd gone on our date… or dates. But something told me that would be a very bad idea.

"I'm just having coffee," I said. "Black."

"I'll have the steak burger, fries and a chocolate malted," Donna said.

"Whipped cream?"

"Why not?"

Gwen scribbled on her pad, repeated our orders, then tore the guest check from her pad and set it face down on the table and went away. I watched her cross the room to the kitchen and go through the double doors, then I turned back to Donna and lifted my eyebrows. Donna slouched back in the booth and looked out at the parking lot.

I was glad to see her order something. I was worried she was becoming anorexic or something, she was so thin. Or maybe she just took after me. All skin and bones.

Anyway, anorexia was likely the least of her problems. A young kid like her—from a broken home, with a creepy stepfather, no friends—she was a prime candidate for trouble, the kind of girl destined to get knocked up at fifteen or sixteen by some lowlife punk. It made me think of that black kid who used to hang around the house, sniffing around Donna like an alley cat. Grady. Eddie Grady. There were only three black boys in the whole town, and one of them had to have the hots for my little girl. I finally had to run the little bastard off. He went, but not without first calling me a racist honky and threatening to burn my house down. That really pissed me off. I mean, I'm no more racist than the next guy.

That got me thinking about my house again, and my mood tanked suddenly.

Gwen brought my coffee and said our food would be right up. She even gave me a little smile. Maybe she wasn't pissed after all. I looked at her ring finger, and there was a ring. Oh well.

After she left, I said, "So how are you getting along with—"

"—What if I moved in with you?" Donna cut in.

Woah. That came out of left field. I took a long drag on my smoke while my brain tried to process this new proposition. I had given a little more thought to Frank staying with me once I found a cheap apartment or some shotgun shack to rent, but not Donna. What the hell did I know about raising teenage girls? What did anybody know about it?

"I'm kind of staying in this fleabag motel right now—"

"What about after you get a place? You *are* gonna get a place here, ain't you? You can't live in a motel the rest of your life."

I groped through the dark corners of my mind, searching for a way out, but I kept bumping into the usual walls and heavy furniture. "What about staying with your sister for a while?" I said.

"I already asked her. She said no."

Of course she would say that. Rose had her own life now; she wanted nothing more to do with us. She'd worked hard for her solid, middle-class existence—God knows the things she'd done to get it—and the rest of us weren't going to do anything to screw it up for her.

I crushed out my cigarette. "We'll see. Maybe once I get settled. Maybe you and your brother—"

"When's that gonna be?"

"Hard to say. Once I get on my feet."

She folded her arms and slumped against the back of the booth. "And when's that gonna be?"

"Soon as I find a job, and save up for a deposit on an apartment, first and last month. Maybe I'll rent a little bungalow, or a cottage by the lake."

"What lake?"

"It's just an expression."

"Can't you get your old job back?"

I took a sip of coffee. "Not likely."

Gwen arrived with Donna's food and refilled my coffee. The smile was gone from her face. Donna squirted some ketchup on her plate, then she picked up a French fry and dragged it listlessly through the puddle of ketchup.

"Russ is such a creep. The way he looks at me… Makes my skin crawl."

I paused my coffee in mid-air. "How's he look at you?"

Donna stared at her plate. "Can we not talk about him?"

"You tell him he touches you, I'll kill him."

"If he touches me, I'll kill him."

There was a lull. I watched my daughter pick at her food. The steakburger sat untouched. She'd had, at most, two sips of the malted.

"Sandy says he's got money—"

"Russ?"

"You'd never know it. He dresses like a hobo." She glanced up at me. "You ever seen his house?"

I nodded. I knew Russ' place—a standard 1920's working-class house. Small, three-bedroom Craftsman bungalow. Hadn't changed since the day it was built. Still had the original wallpaper and a big old clawfoot tub and a toilet with the tank way up on the wall. Rooms were dark and musty with big heavy curtains blocking out the sunlight, like he was farming mushrooms in there.

"You should hear the horrible, disgusting noises he makes. Sits in front of the TV belching and farting and sucking his teeth."

I laughed. I couldn't help myself.

"You think it's funny?"

This old couple sitting nearby turned their heads and gave us a perturbed look. I leaned across the table and whispered, "Old people are staring at us."

"If he's got money, he's sure good at hiding it. The only nice thing I ever saw is that stupid car of his, the one he never drives."

I'd forgotten about the car, the one real love of Russ' life. A '57 T-bird. Fire engine red. I'd had a glimpse of it a few times, always parked in his backyard garage. Come to think of it, I'd never seen him drive the car either. Probably afraid it would get dirty or scratched if he took it out on the street.

"What's the point of having a car like that if all you do is keep it in mothballs?" Donna said.

I shrugged and sipped my coffee. "He's an odd duck. Who else decides he wants to make his fortune pumping out other people's crap?"

"Frank says he's got like two or three thousand dollars in rare coins in his desk. One of these days, he's gonna swipe them and hitchhike to Alaska and never come back."

"Frank is?"

"Uh-huh."

"To Alaska?"

Donna nodded.

"Really? Frank said that?"

She took a sip of her malted.

"Sounds cold," I said.

Donna shuddered and looked out the window. "Gotta be better than this."

I took a last sip of coffee and picked up the check. "He needs to stay here and finish school. Both of you do."

She pushed her plate away. She hadn't even touched the burger. "You should talk. *You* never finished high school. Sandy neither."

"Exactly. You want to end up like us?"

"Hell no." She sat quietly for a while. Then she lifted her eyes toward me and said, "So, what about it?"

"What about what?"

She let out a loud, exasperated sigh. "About me staying with you?"

I studied the check and said, "We'll see. Maybe once I get settled in. If your mother allows it."

Her face puckered to a scowl. "She'll never agree to that."

"I'll talk to her."

I left Gwen a buck tip, and we slid out of the booth and made our way to the register. I handed the ticket to some poor schlump wearing a Christmas tie and a silly Santa Claus cap at the register. The manager, I assumed. He gave us a greasy smile and said, "How was everything?"

"Terrific. Excellent service." I pulled out my wallet and handed him ten bucks.

Donna said, "God, I can't wait till I'm old enough to get my own place."

"You'll be eighteen before you know it."

"No way. I'm getting emancipated as soon as I turn sixteen."

"Emancipated? What are you talking about… like the slaves? What are you, a slave?"

"I'm serious. Kelly's older sister did it when she turned seventeen."

"Kelly who?"

"Never mind. You don't know her. You don't know any of my friends."

She had me there. I didn't think she had any friends. I pocketed my change and said, "Don't you have to go to court for that? Hire a lawyer and whatnot?"

"So? I'll get a job and pay the stupid lawyer."

It sounded like she'd been thinking about this emancipation business for a while. Oh well, she was only fourteen. Or was she thirteen? Anyway, she'd forget all about it soon enough.

I looked for Gwen. I wanted to say goodbye or give her a smile or something, but she was busy with customers.

As we walked across the parking lot, I turned to Donna and said, "Hey, I almost forgot to ask you what you want for Christmas?"

She didn't even look at me. "Cash, for my emancipation fund."

"I was thinking a sweater," I said. "How about a nice sweater?"

"Cash."

As she walked on ahead of me to the station wagon, I remember thinking, Now there goes a girl who knows what she wants.

FIVE

I WAS GIVEN A SPONSOR, a fellow by the name of Greg Schikler. He looked to be about my age, but after that, the similarities ended. Greg Schikler didn't strike me as a guy who had drinking problems—or any kind of problems. Greg Schikler seemed like a fella who had his head on straight and his shit together. He drove a '69 Jaguar convertible, mint condition. I mean, if you're driving a car like that, how messed up can your life be?

It took me a while to put two and two together. *Schikler. Schikler.* Then it came to me. The name was everywhere. His family was one of the biggest real estate developers in the region. You couldn't miss their signs: The Schikler Group. Cruise down any suburban highway in the Midwest and you'll drive past their handiwork: big box shopping centers anchored by K-Marts and Ventures with enough parking for a dozen cruise ships. No wonder the guy drove a vintage sports car.

We met for the first time at a little café downtown, one of the few businesses still operating down there. I suppose rent was cheap since three-quarters of the shops were empty—the small mom and pops having been run out of business when the new mall opened. I parked on an empty downtown street and walked a few blocks to the cafe, past a former jeweler, a former

SO MANY THINGS TO BURY

bank, a former clothing store, a former barber shop, a former drugstore with a former lunch counter, a former hardware store, and a former movie theater—now serving as some kind of bogus, storefront Church—the sign of a dead downtown if ever there was one. All that was missing was a tumbleweed blowing past and the screech of a golden eagle.

The diner bore the highly original name of Downtown Café. Inside were a half dozen folks, most of whom looked like they'd gotten lost looking for the Salvation Army Soup Kitchen, or maybe they'd drifted in to get out of the cold. I found Greg scribbling away at one of the back tables. He looked up, grinned, and hopped to his feet when he saw me. He stuck out his hand, but when he saw my bandages, he gave my arm a friendly squeeze instead. He didn't ask about my hand.

"How about a cup of joe, Al?"

"No thanks. Never touch the stuff."

"Tea then? Something to eat? They got a real nice menu here. You ought to try the reuben, it's out of this world, if I do say so myself."

"No thanks, really." None of that sounded good. The only thing that sounded good at the moment was a double shot of Early Times and a Marlboro, but I kept that to myself. For some reason, I wanted to make a good impression.

Greg went back to fetch his coffee, which was already in a to-go cup. "How would you feel about taking a walk? Unless it's too cold for you?"

I shrugged. "It's not too cold."

"Great, then. A little fresh air."

We strode past an old Irish pub that had somehow managed to survive the retail apocalypse—bars and churches. They're like cockroaches in their indestructibility. I gazed longingly at the pub's dark windows and beat-up front door as we plodded on. Greg caught me looking at the pub and said, "So, Al, how're you holding up?"

"Honestly? I could use a drink."

"Well sure. A totally normal feeling—and sadly one that never completely goes away. I can attest to that. Just when you think you've got it beat, the damn cravings come back with a vengeance and, *Bam!* Knock you on your ass."

We stood at the corner of Third and Locust waiting for the light to change, even though there wasn't a single car in view. This Schikler was apparently a stickler when it came to following rules. Maybe there was something to be said for rule-following. Maybe if I'd followed the rules, I'd be driving a vintage Jaguar too.

Followed the rules and inherited a million bucks from a rich uncle.

"You know what I do when it gets really bad?" Greg said. He didn't wait for my response. "I try to get the focus off me. I try to do something for somebody else, you know? See if I can't do a good turn for somebody. Ever hear the phrase, 'Ego is the enemy?' You see what I'm saying? It's all about getting the focus off me, and directing it toward others."

I gazed at the flashing orange DON'T WALK sign, which kept blinking like crazy even though there wasn't a car within ten miles. "Yeah, well, that sounds good and all, but I'm not so sure the enemy is ego, as much as… you know… booze. And all the shit you're trying to numb with the booze."

"Sure, sure," Greg said. "Alcohol is, well, the way I like to look at it, it's sort of neutral. It doesn't have any agency, you know what I mean? It can't hurt us unless we let it. And if we're looking outside ourselves, it's harder for the alcohol to have an impact."

I wasn't sure what he was talking about, and besides, I was getting tired of this conversation. "Anyway," I said, "thanks for doing this. Sponsoring me, I mean. I really do appreciate it."

"That's the reason we're here, right? To help each other?"

I shrugged. That sounded good, but if that was true, I was really falling down on the job. I wasn't even helping my own family. Not much anyway.

The light changed. As we started across the street, I cleared my throat and said, "Mind if I ask you a personal question?"

Greg nodded slightly. "Sure. Go ahead, buddy."

"You've been sober how long?"

"Four years," he said, giving an easy smile. "Four years, two months and...twenty-one days to be exact."

"So... when does it start getting easier?"

Greg considered for a moment. "I wouldn't say it ever gets easier, but you sort of get used to it. I guess it's like being a combat soldier. It's always hell, but after a while you can get used to hell. Does that make any sense?"

"Mostly it's boredom."

"What is?"

"Being a combat soldier."

"Oh... sure," he said.

"No offense, Greg, but you don't particularly strike me as someone who is going through hell."

"Not on the outside, maybe."

I gave a small grunt of acknowledgement.

"Like I said, you get used to it." After a thoughtful silence, Greg said, "Tell me something, Al. Why do you want to get sober? I mean, the real, honest-to-God reason."

For some reason, his question rubbed me the wrong way, and I responded ill-temperedly. "That's kind of a dumb thing to ask, ain't it? Kind of like asking a cancer patient why he wants to be cured of cancer?"

Greg gave me a knowing look. "Except a person with cancer can't decide to stop having cancer." He studied me for a moment. "If it's too personal, just say so. Just tell me to mind my own business. It won't hurt my feelings at all." When I didn't say anything, he went on: "I've been going to A.A. meetings for nine years—off and on—and one thing I've learned is no two alcoholics are alike. Everyone's got his own story and his own reasons for wanting to get sober."

"No, I get it." I felt bad for snapping at him. He was only

trying to help. A wealthy guy like Greg could have been doing a thousand better things with his time. Sailing the Greek Islands. Skiing in the Alps. Whatever. And yet here he was, walking the empty streets of a dead downtown, trying to give hope to a miserable son of a bitch like me.

"I don't mind talking about it," I said. "I guess... well, I lost my wife, I lost my kids, my house, my job. You might say I'm running out of things to lose."

"So you hope that by getting sober you'll get those things back?"

"I'm not getting my wife back, and the house has already been sold. I'm not gonna get my old job back either. I don't know, maybe the kids wouldn't hate me so much if I turned over a new leaf. If they saw I was trying, anyway."

Greg nodded. "Nothing more important than your kids."

"You can always get another job. Another house. Hell, another wife."

We shared a laugh at that.

"Well, that ain't exactly true," I said. "My granddaddy's house really was one of a kind. Built it with his own two hands. Another house would be... ya know... just another house."

Greg tossed his empty coffee cup into a trash can as we stood waiting pointlessly at another traffic light. Neither one of us said anything for a while, then I nodded toward the traffic signal. "You got some pull at city hall, don't you, Greg? Why not get rid of these lights? And these parking meters while you're at it? What the hell's the point?"

"Oh, I don't know. I think downtown's gonna come back. Maybe not like before, but it'll reinvent itself. It's happening all over the country, downtowns reinventing themselves. Little specialty stores, antique shops, cafes, bars, bookstores, places that sell that homemade soap and candles and stuff. Old women love that crap. That's one thing old downtowns got that malls don't—these charming old brick buildings and the walkable streets. Of course, you got to fix them up before they're charming again, and that doesn't come cheap. The people who want to open antique shops and bookstores usually don't have a lot of money, so you've got to figure a way to get the taxpayers to pitch in."

The light flashed WALK, and we started across the street. I said, "I guess you're kind of to blame for this, ain't you?"

I guess I was feeling a little ornery. Who wouldn't? Nobody likes to feel small in front of another man, and that's what it feels like having your A.A. sponsor following you around, asking a lot of personal questions, telling you how you should live your life. Greg gave me a look like he wasn't quite sure where I was going with this.

"Funny, you guys built the mall out there on the interstate," I said. "This must be like coming back to the scene of the crime."

Greg's face had darkened perceptibly. "I wasn't involved with the mall," he said evenly. "Nor was my family."

"I thought I saw your name—"

"Some of the shopping centers out there, yes. The Wal-Mart. The Venture. But not the mall."

I shrugged. "Okay."

Greg slowed his step. I guess he couldn't keep up his rapid pace and defend his business ethics at the same time.

"I'm not exactly sure how we got on this topic, but I will say this: My conscience is clear. What you got to understand, Al, is that times change. This kind of thing is happening all over the country. Hell, the world. What're you gonna do? You can't stop progress."

I said, "I guess I never thought of Wal-Mart as progress."

"What would you call it, then?"

I thought about that. "Godzilla?"

"Huh?"

"I'd call something that destroys downtown Godzilla."

We walked on in silence. I must have hit a sore spot. I didn't really care one way or another what happened to downtown—it wasn't like I had a job or a business down there—but I was sort of enjoying tweaking Greg's guilty conscience. It's not every day a poor son of a bitch like me gets to stick it to one of the town's elites.

"That café we met at," he said. "You know it's mine."

"No kidding? No wonder it can afford to stay open." I figured I had the knife in, I might as well go ahead and give it a little twist. "I get it now," I said. "You feel guilty about killing off downtown, so this café is like... whatcha call it... *penance*."

Greg gave me a hard stare. "I don't feel guilty, Al. But I do want to help downtown succeed. And it will. But like I said, it's not gonna be major department stores and retail chains. No, it'll be a destination."

"Destination? This place?"

"That's right. Quirky little shops, cafes, coffeehouses, record stores. Maybe even an art theater."

"The kind of quirky little places that go out of business in six months."

Greg sighed. "Why don't we talk about something else?"

"Okay by me."

We didn't seem to be heading anywhere in particular, just the depressing grand tour of a once-thriving downtown. I thought that maybe I'd gone too far with the needling, when Greg said, "You haven't told me how you like the meetings so far?"

"I'm gonna level with you, Greg. I'm not completely sold on A.A.. It's a bit churchy for me. My people have never been very religious, and all that Jesus stuff kinda makes my skin crawl."

Greg laughed. "Yeah, a lot of people get hung up on that higher power stuff, but to be honest, it's really not about that."

"Good to know. What's it about then?"

"It's more about giving up the notion that we have control, because we don't."

I didn't see the difference. Probably I'm too stupid. "So, you're saying *God* has control."

"Maybe nobody has control," he said. "A lot of people look at me, and they think, there's a guy who's got it under control."

Greg shook his head. "Wouldn't they be surprised."

"Then they ought to get rid of it—all that superstitious mumbo jumbo."

Greg smiled. "A lot of people like the 'mumbo jumbo.'"

I looked away. "I don't know."

"Just give it a chance, huh?"

"Sure," I said. "It's not like I got a plan B."

As we walked on, my thoughts kept turning back to what we'd been discussing earlier—the old homestead and it being gone forever. There was no getting over the fact that we were losing the family home on my watch, and it made me feel like a total loser. It wasn't right. It wasn't fair. Even a kid like Donna could see how messed up it all was. And who stood to benefit? My lousy cousin Russ. The bastard would make a nice profit from the sale.

Greg clapped me on the back, snapping me out of my reverie.

"I will say this, Al. I like you. I do. Our first get-together and already you're busting my balls about these empty storefronts. I'm not saying you're right, but I like a man who isn't shy about speaking his mind. One thing I can't stand is an ass kisser. I can't tell you how many ass kissers I meet in my line of work. You never know what people are really thinking, if they're just trying to figure out what you want them to say or what. People like that are worse than useless. That's why I like you, Al. You tell it straight."

I couldn't see what he was getting at. Here I thought I'd offended him, but the bastard seemed to enjoy being insulted. Maybe he was some kind of masochist.

We came to the next corner and again cooled our heels till we got the WALK sign. Greg brought out a pack of Wrigley's Doublemint, unwrapped a stick, and offered the pack to me. I said no thanks.

"Mark my word," Greg said, waving toward the rows of empty shops. "Five years from now, most of these storefronts will be occupied, then we'll have all kinds of holiday festivities down here. Parades and Santa Claus and what have you. Just like the old days."

"If you say so."

"Ten years tops."

I wondered if he was going to buy up all the empty storefronts himself and fill them up with comic book stores. Not that I gave a damn one way or another.

"That's another nice thing about downtowns," he went on. "You can't really have a Santa Claus parade in the parking lot of a Wal-Mart. You need a downtown for that."

"A *flourishing* downtown, you mean."

"Right."

"Not a dead one."

We crossed the empty street in silence, sticking to the sunny side of the street, which had less snow, but more slush. Greg looked at me side-eyed and said, "So, Al, you mentioned kids. How many have you got, if you don't mind my asking?"

I fumbled in my work jacket for my pack of cigarettes. "Three. Two girls and a boy."

"Yeah? I got two boys and a girl. Love 'em to death. 'Course, I only get to see them every other weekend, which kinda sucks. But it could be worse, right?"

Yeah, I thought. You could also be dirt poor.

Ahead loomed the one downtown department store that was still open, sort of, a JC Penny with Going-Out-Of-Business banners hung over the display windows. It reminded me I still hadn't gotten the kids anything for Christmas. What was it Donna wanted?

That's right. Cash. For a lawyer.

We passed the old Santa hut out front of the Penny's, the same one my mother had taken me and Leroy and Anna to when we were kids. From the looks of it, Santa had fallen on hard times too. The paint on his house was cracked and peeling and much of the wood had rotted away. Santa appeared to be MIA. Probably out at the new mall like everybody else, or passed out under a table at the Irish pub. Stupidly, I made eye contact with a panhandler hanging out in front of the Santa hut, and he made a beeline in our direction. The bums sure had slim pickings downtown, but I guess it was hard for them to get way the hell out to the shopping centers, or maybe the folks who run the mall are good about running them off.

"What d'ya say we head back?" I said. The last thing I felt like doing was getting into a long, sad conversation with a bum.

"Excuse me!" the panhandler cried. He hurried over and drew up alongside us, matching us step for step. One thing I've noticed about panhandlers—they are quick on their feet. Too bad they don't put that energy to use doing something productive. This fella looked like he was about forty with not a thing in the world wrong with him, except that he was forty years old and had no self-respect. Greg stopped, so I had no choice but to stop, too. The beggar stuck out his hand, and Greg clasped it like they were bosom buddies. Then he went to shake my hand, but I was having none of that. I got a thing about shaking hands with tramps, and I sure as hell ain't going to do it when my hand is all bandaged up. After I left him hanging, the panhandler ignored me and went to work on Greg, spinning his tale of woe, how he couldn't get a job no matter where he tried, not even at the McDonalds. His wife needed a new kidney, or a used kidney anyway, and neither one of them had had a decent meal in weeks, and as for these food pantries, they only got canned goods and do you know how much salt is in canned goods? Enough for ten heart attacks. He asked Greg if he knew how long it'd been since his wife had had any meat, which sounded to me like the setup to a dirty joke.

"Two months," he said. "I'm no bum. Check this out. Are you a fan of the king?"

"You mean Elvis?" Greg said.

The bum flipped up his collar and karate kicked the air. Then he began butchering the opening lines to *Baby Let's Play House*.

"Woah baby, baby, baby, baby..."

I had farts that sounded more like Elvis than this guy.

"Hey, you're pretty good," Greg said.

I cleared my throat and told Greg that I needed to get back. Greg nodded and reached for his wallet. "What kind of cut does your wife like?" Greg asked the panhandler.

"Huh?"

"Rib eye? Sirloin tips? Filet mignon?"

"Oh, whatever's fine. She's not too particular."

Greg handed over a twenty-dollar bill. Just like that. Twenty bucks.

The tramp said, "Thank ya, thank ya very much," and pumped Greg's hand again and turned and ran off after the next pigeon.

I shook my head. "Do you give every panhandler you meet twenty bucks?"

Greg looked at me squarely. "Sometimes, I just listen to them. Sometimes that's all they need—a friendly ear."

"Not that guy. That guy needed a bottle of Mad Dog 20/20. And he ain't the only one."

Greg gave me a sympathizing look. All I could do was shrug.

We started back. We actually caught a few WALK signals this time. Suddenly, Greg stopped in his tracks and snapped his fingers. "I know what I wanted to ask you. You live alone, right?"

I nodded.

"An apartment?"

"At the moment, I'm staying at this charming fleabag motel down the road. Suicides rave about the place. Why d'ya ask?"

"Do you mind a little pro tip?"

"Um..."

"When a man's trying to remain sober, he doesn't want to be alone. It's too easy to get bored and depressed and yield to temptation. You see what I'm saying?"

He wasn't telling me anything I didn't already know, nothing

I hadn't heard at a dozen A.A. meetings.

"Are your parents still living?"

"My mother. Though I wouldn't call what she does living."

Greg smiled. "Would she let you stay with her for a while?"

"My mother? My mother lives in this little apartment the size of a walk-in closet."

"Is she a drinker?"

"I wouldn't say that. Her vice is cigarettes. Three or four packs a day."

"Would she let you move in with her for a while?"

"She lives in this senior housing complex full of old women."

"No offense, but that sounds nicer than your motel."

He had me there.

"I'm telling you, Al, you've got a much better chance of beating this if you're not on your own. All the better if you're surrounded by little old ladies. It wouldn't be forever. Just six months or so."

"*Just* six months?" I shook my head. "If you only knew my mother... Anyway, she would never agree to that."

"Couldn't hurt to ask, right?"

I considered that. "It would definitely hurt, but I'll think about it."

"That's all I ask."

Greg checked his watch (a gold Rolex, from the looks of it) and said he had to meet a client. He gave my arm a friendly squeeze and said we should get together again soon, then he turned and headed toward his roadster. I watched him get in, wave, and drive off.

It was then that I decided to burn my house down.

Six

IF I WAS SERIOUS about keeping straight, I was going to have to do something desperate, and what could be more desperate than a middle-aged man moving in with his surly, nicotine-and-television-addicted mother? Or more sad.

Ma wasn't exactly overjoyed to see me. That was no surprise. I'd never been her favorite. That title belonged to my older brother who'd been killed in the South Pacific—in The Good War. Leroy, the military hero, hadn't lived long enough to disappoint my parents. He never became the sad, shell-shocked, divorced drunk that we all became. Ma had conveniently forgotten that the reason Leroy had gone into the Marines in the first place was on account of him getting caught stealing tires off cars in the lot of a Cadillac dealership. A county judge gave him the choice of a year at the work camp or a stint in the Marines. Leroy really wanted to do the year at the camp because you don't usually get your arms and legs and balls blown off at a work camp, while the Marines gig could be for the duration of the war and nobody knew how long that would be, not even the geniuses who were supposedly calling the shots. Our old man was so angered by my brother's lack of patriotism that he slapped Leroy in the face right in front of the judge, called Leroy a goddamn coward, and said he was ashamed of him, ashamed to be his father. Then the old man turned to the judge and said the boy would be proud to serve in the Marines if they would have him. The judge stared at my father for a moment. "Don't ever touch anyone in my courtroom again," the judge said. After that, we all went home, except my brother who went to Okinawa to die.

I stood at the mantel studying Leroy's official armed services portrait, which was arranged in a place of honor beside a framed burial flag. Leroy smirking in his dress blues, posing in front of Old Glory.

My official Army portrait was nowhere to be seen.

I took a seat in the old wooden rocker that had belonged to my late great grandmother. Ma turned and gave me a blank look, then went back to her cigarette and TV show. Christ, her place looked even more depressing than I remembered. Beside her on the couch sat a green glass ashtray that looked like it had never been emptied. The same stunted artificial Christmas tree leaned in one corner of the room atop an antique end table as it had every Christmas for the past ten years. From a dirty cage behind the couch, a pair of goldfinches leapt perch to perch. I couldn't figure out how those birds had survived so long in that toxic environment. They didn't so much sing or tweet as hack and wheeze.

Neither of us seemed in the mood for small talk, and I wasn't sure how to work up to things, so I got straight to the point. "Got a favor to ask you, Ma."

"I bet you do. Can't it wait till a commercial?"

I shook my head wearily and got up and went into the kitchenette and got myself a cup of coffee. The coffee tasted cold and stale, so I poured it down the drain.

Ma coughed a good long while, then she said, "Did you come over here to waste my coffee? D'you think coffee grows on trees?"

"I'm pretty sure it does."

"Shhhhh!"

I picked up the newspaper and sat down at the little kitchen table and went over the sports pages. I wasn't much of a sports fan. Most guys get their love of sports from their fathers, but my old man thought sports was childish nonsense and a waste of a man's time, so rather than tossing a ball around the yard with his kids he spent his time playing gin rummy with his work buddies.

Some time passed. I folded the newspaper and dropped it on the chair. Ever since we'd run into that Elvis-impersonating panhandler, that tune *Baby Let's Play House* had been kicking around in my head—especially the line where Elvis says *I'd rather see my baby dead than see her with another man.*

I guess that's how I felt about things. Not about my ex-wife; I don't mean that. I mean about the house. Hell, Russ could have Sandy—take her with my blessing, but nobody was getting the family home but family.

The show went to a commercial. Ma hacked up a piece of lung, then she turned and studied me for a long moment. "What did you say you wanted?"

"Nice seeing you, too."

"Don't give me that. You only come round here when you want something. Money usually. Well, you're too late. I gave it all to the Sunday Morning Gospel Hour."

"Since when do you watch that shit?"

"Since I got saved. Since I accepted Jesus as my personal savior. Since I was washed in the blood of the lamb."

"You're so full of shit. You don't have any money to give away."

"What are you doing here? I thought you were living in Florida?"

"Texas. I was living in Texas—and no. I mean, I don't know."

"You don't know where you're living?"

I stared at my feet. "That's what I wanted to talk to you about."

Another commercial came on, an ad for bug spray. Raid.

Kills bugs dead.

"I take it you ain't working."

"I was till I got laid off."

"You mean fired," she said. "You know your wife moved in with Russ Berger."

"I know."

"What kind of woman does that... moves in with her husband's cousin?"

I didn't say anything. Mom had never been a big fan of Sandy or her family. They weren't of German stock. They were Scotch-Irish something—one of them "inferior" races.

Anyway...

"What happened to you?" She was studying my bandaged hand. Even when she tried to show genuine motherly concern, it somehow sounded like an accusation.

"Nothing. A dog bite."

"Dog bite, hell. You put your fist through a winda, didn't ya?"

"What do you got somebody tailing me?"

She made a face and let it drop. "I hear you sold our home."

I rubbed my hand over my face. I swear there was a goddamn mole in the family. "It wasn't my idea, trust me."

"When were you gonna tell me?"

"I figured you already knew. You seem to know everything."

"It's a good thing your father isn't alive to hear about this. It would've killed him. Your grandfather built that house. Built it from scratch."

"I know, ma."

"Shhhh, my show's coming on."

That started me thinking about my old man. Thinking how if my mother had divorced him and tried to make him sell the house... I don't know what he would have done. I couldn't see him going along with it, though. I could see him putting a bullet in the back of her head. He could be an ornery son of a bitch when he got liquored up.

I thought about that—all the ways my old man might have

murdered her—till the show ended, then I got up and snapped off the television set.

"Who said you could turn off my set?" Ma snapped.

"So, what would you think if I moved in here for a while?"

The question struck her momentarily dumb. Her mummified mouth hung open like it'd come off its hinges. "Move in here? This place?" She busied herself removing a cigarette from her pack and lighting it with a chrome lighter. "You're not serious."

"I know it sounds crazy—"

"You're damn right it's crazy. You're a grown-ass man. You got a family. Well, had a family."

"I still have—"

"Speaking of which, when am I gonna see them grandkids of mine? I haven't seen hide nor hair of 'em since… hell, I can't remember the last time I saw 'em. Maybe I should just give up ever seeing them again. I warned you this would happen when you married one of them people."

She was obviously trying to change the subject, or piss me off, hoping I'd get angry enough to storm out so she could go back to her TV and cigarettes.

I said, "I'll bring them over on Christmas Day."

"I won't hold my breath." Her eyes slid around the room, then fixed on me again. "Moving into this tiny apartment. Lord, what would the other residents think? Alma Freivogal's son is taking her on a Caribbean cruise next month, and here my son is asking to shack up with me."

I felt sick to my stomach. What the hell was I thinking, taking advice from a rich bastard like Greg? What did he know about the problems of the working poor? Or in my case, the non-working poor.

"You know what? Forget it. I'm sorry I asked."

I got to my feet.

Ma started into coughing again, a good, long jag. She held out a hand to stay me till she could speak again.

"You never did tell me where you're staying. You ain't

sleeping in your car, are you? Lord, that would really be the end. Here Mandy Krodel's daughter just bought her a brand-new color TV and my homeless son's sleeping in his station wagon."

"I got a room."

"Then why do you want to move in here?"

"It's about drying out."

"Drying out." She spat out the words like venom. "You can't dry out in your own place?"

"They say it works better if you're not alone. If you got some... moral support." I couldn't believe how ridiculous I sounded.

Ma laughed bitterly. "You mean someone nagging you all the time? Like I used to nag your father for drinking? Drinking and gambling. Gambling and drinking. No thanks, I've had my bellyful of that. Besides, it don't work. Didn't work with him, and it won't work with his son."

I was wasting my time. Maybe if I had brought her a gift or something. A carton of Pall Malls. Why didn't I ever think of gifts? Why was I so goddamn self-centered? I glanced around the room through the gray smog of second-hand smoke at the worn-out furniture, the heavy urine-colored curtains, probably white at one time. Everything reeking of stale cigarette smoke. I had forgotten how tiny the apartment was. Far too cramped for two adults.

I zipped up my jacket. "Sorry I bothered you." I went over and turned on the television set.

Ma's voice came up behind me. "Now just hold your horses."

I paused.

"How long?"

"What?"

"How long were you thinking?"

I kept my eyes fixed on the screen, a game show with people dressed like it was Halloween, jumping around like they were having a fit. "Six months or so."

"Six months!"

"Maybe less."

She muttered something I didn't catch. Then, "What about a job? Think you're going to lie around here all day watching TV?"

"I'll find something. Might take a few weeks."

I could hear a telephone ringing in a downstairs apartment. Ma stared blankly at the television screen. After a moment, she said, "Where are you staying now?"

"Shaw's Motel."

"That dump?"

"A dump would be an improvement."

I waited a moment longer, and when she said nothing more, I moved toward the door. I couldn't wait to get out of there.

Ma cleared her throat. "You're really serious about this? About getting straight?"

I paused, my hand on the doorknob. "You think I'd come begging like this if I wasn't?"

"Your father went on the wagon more times than I can count. Fell off every goddamn time. I finally told him to quit kidding himself."

"Merry Christmas, ma." I opened the door and stepped out into the hallway, out into the stale potpourri-scented air, and shut the door behind me. I was actually relieved I wouldn't be staying with her. We probably would have killed each other. One of them murder-suicides—though it was a toss-up who'd kill who first. I was halfway to the stairs when I heard the door creak open.

"I'll give you three months."

That stopped me.

"You can stay three months—on the pull-out couch. If you're not dried out by then, you ain't never gonna be." She paused and said, "And I expect you to pay half the rent."

I took a deep breath and let it out slowly. "I'll get my things," I said.

SEVEN

I WENT BACK TO the motel and started packing. Not that I had much to pack, except a few dirty socks and some dirty underwear. I dragged my footlocker around to the side of the bed and took out the false bottom where I'd hidden the cigar box with my cash. You couldn't be too careful in these welfare motels, though I doubt that cardboard bottom would have fooled a blind man on a dark night. I peeled off five one-hundred-dollar bills, put back the cigar box and covered it up with some clothes, then I put the suitcase on top of the footlocker. I gave the room one last look. Something streaked behind the dresser, a small gray blur. I picked up my things and lugged them out the door.

After I packed up the station wagon, I went down to the motel office. The place was empty. I cleared my throat loudly a few times, then I clapped the bell. The fat lady who seemed to be in charge slowly worked her way out of the back room on her two canes. After she'd plopped down on a stool, I told her I'd changed my mind about staying the week and asked about a refund for the other six nights.

She gave me a look like I'd spit in her eye. "What's the matter? You don't like the room?"

"I like it fine. Not as much as the rodents, maybe. The thing is, I got other plans."

"You saw a rat?"
"I think it was a large mouse."
"Did you kill it?"
"What? No, I didn't kill... What am I, pest control?"
She didn't say anything to that.
"So how about that refund?"
"You can't read?" She turned and taped one of her canes against the framed NO REFUNDS sign tacked to the wall behind her. I hadn't noticed the sign.
"But I only stayed one night—"
"Rules is rules," she said and slowly got to her feet. Then she turned on her canes and moved like a glacier toward the back room.

I stood there a moment, trying to think of something smart to say, but nothing came to me. I didn't know what else to do, so I left.

I walked the block to the phone booth and flipped through the phone book till I found the number of a guy I used to work with at the VW car dealership two or three years ago. I wasn't sure he was still alive. A guy like that, chances were fifty-fifty, at best. I let the phone ring a long time. One of the few things I remember about Mike Barker was he didn't care for telephones. Make that he *hated* telephones. It was like a phobia or something with him. I believe he had a telephone, but he almost never used it. He preferred to talk in person. If he wanted to talk to you, he'd drive over to your house and do it face-to-face—"like a human being"—he'd say, whatever that meant. He never told me why he hated telephones so much and I didn't care enough to ask. If I had to guess, I'd bet it had something to do with the police bugging his phone, or, more likely, him *imagining* that the police were bugging his phone.

Barker answered on the ninth ring. He remembered me immediately, even though a lot of years had passed and we had never been tight. He hadn't remained at the dealership long enough for us to get tight. After some catching up, I asked him if he was looking to make a nice piece of change for an hour's work.

"I could be," he said, "but nothing illegal, because YOU KNOW I NEVER DO NOTHIN' ILLEGAL!"

That was obviously for the benefit of the FBI or whoever he imagined was listening in.

"No, it's strictly above board," I said. "But we should probably discuss it in person."

I asked him when he could meet, and he said he wasn't doing anything now. He suggested we meet at a bar, probably hoping he could get a few free drinks out of the deal. I didn't want to meet at a bar for obvious reasons. I finally convinced Barker to go someplace less public, some place we wouldn't be overheard. He suggested his house. I said somebody might see my car there and that could come back to bite us in the ass. I was starting to think I'd picked the wrong arsonist when he finally agreed to meet at the city park on the south side of town.

Citizens Park wasn't so much a park as a collection of sports fields and baseball diamonds, dormant in winter, with a small iced-over pond and one low-rent picnic area. Lots of weeds and grasses, but very few trees. I parked just up the hill from the pond and had a cigarette while I waited. Twenty minutes passed and there was still no sign of Barker. I was getting jumpy.

I hadn't seen Barker since the day they fired him from the car dealership for stealing automotive tools. Turns out he was the reason you could never find a socket wrench when you needed one. Barker—who was probably 22, give or take a couple of years—had only worked in the garage four months before he got canned. God knows how much stuff he walked off with during that time. Another two months, and he probably would've picked the shop clean. I thought the chances were good a shitbum like Barker would be out of work and desperate for some quick cash and would do pretty much anything to get it. As long as it was quick and easy and paid well. What I had planned would be as easy as falling off a telephone pole.

I had a damn good reason for not wanting to go to Barker's house. I'd been to his place once before, about a week before he got the sack. Back then he was always trying to get me to come over after work and drink with him, maybe smoke a little weed or what have you. I have no idea why he asked me. Maybe everybody else had already told the little creep to get lost. I kept putting him off, till I finally ran out of excuses. A normal person would get the hint after being told three dozen times that I wasn't feeling well or that I had to visit my mother in the hospital or that I had tickets to The Nutcracker. Not Barker.

He finally wore me down.

I'd expected to drive up to some burned out single wide trailer, but he actually lived in a pretty nice old farmhouse down a long unpaved road. There wasn't a neighbor in sight. He'd moved in after his grandmother died. Died of what? I wondered. Impatient Grandson Syndrome? I got the impression that he wasn't the rightful occupier of the farmhouse, that he was squatting there, and that someday, after the real owner sold the place, it would be quite the ordeal dislodging him from the premises—likely involving sheriff's deputies, barricades and a weeks-long stand-off.

The interior of the house wasn't as terrible as I'd expected either. Maybe he hadn't lived there long enough to adequately turn the place upside down. The furniture looked old, but sturdy. Most of the chairs had at least three of their legs. The wood floors were worn and scuffed—but nothing a rug couldn't hide, and the floral wallpaper, though clearly the original wall covering from the Twenties, was only peeling in a couple places. However, if you looked close enough, there were obvious signs that someone like Barker lived there. The walls and ceiling were pockmarked with dozens of small-caliber bullet holes. A frayed and filthy Stars and Bars hung above the fireplace mantle, despite the fact that we lived in Illinois. The fireplace was littered with burned beer cans and broken liquor bottles, and guns were scattered everywhere: rifles, shotguns, semi-automatics, revolvers. More than I could count. For some reason, Barker felt the need to show off each and every firearm, like a boy with his prized baseball card collection.

He tossed me a beer. Then he picked up a Glock and checked to see if it was loaded. "See anything you like?" he asked.

"I don't need a gun."

"Shit man, everybody needs a gun. Numerous guns."

I leaned against the kitchen sink and sipped my beer. "I mean, I already have one."

"Cool. What d'ya got?"

I told him about my souvenir from Korea. A Russian-made Tokarev.

"A commie pistol? No way would I fire that. Piece a shit would probably blow up in my hand. I'd go around the rest of my life with a bloody stump where my hand was."

I was no fan of communist military hardware either, but I was even less of a fan of Barker, which is how I found myself sticking up for The Red Army. "They did kick The Third Reich's ass with those guns."

"The commies? Fuck you talking about? *We* kicked Hitler's ass. The Germans and Japs and Europe and all the rest of 'em. Shit, man, didn't they teach you nothing in school?"

I didn't feel like discussing it anymore.

I hadn't been in Barker's kitchen five minutes before he blew away a cockroach with a Beretta 92. I survived Hwanggan, Poksong-Dong, the fucking Battle of Pusan Perimeter—so not much scares me. But an hour in that hell house with that psychotic son of a bitch had my teeth on edge.

I figured he would be perfect for the job.

I WAITED. I turned on the radio and listened to a local high school basketball game on some grainy AM station. Another five minutes passed before a vehicle with one working headlight rolled up the gravel road. Barker's yellow Dodge Dart—the same one he drove all those years ago—pulled in beside my station wagon and he rolled down the driver's side window and stuck his head out. Smoke billowed through the open window. "Hey Al, good to see ya!"

I snapped off the radio. I eased out of the station wagon and walked over to the Dodge and got in on the passenger side. I could barely see Barker through all the boiling marijuana smoke. A cassette tape played way too loud. I rolled down the window and leaned my head halfway out, trying to breathe some air.

Barker took a long hit off a huge joint and slapped me sharply on the thigh. "Been a while, man," he yelled over the music. Then he coughed a while and turned down the volume on the stereo. "How's the wife and kids? You got three kids, right?"

"They're good. Thanks for asking." I was impressed he remembered. I sure never remember things like that, and I like to think I'm less of a degenerate than he is, so I'm not sure what that says about me. I wasn't sure if Barker had a wife or kids or what. For the sake of humanity, I sure hoped not.

He offered me the joint, and I shook my head. "I'll just breathe in some of this here," I said.

Barker grinned. "You know this is where the queers hang out at night, right?"

"Um, I didn't know that."

"Uh-huh," he said. "So, you still working at the garage? Man, that place sucked hard."

"Yeah, no. I'm between jobs."

"Me too. Between jobs," he said. "So, you mentioned a nice piece of change. I'd like to hear your proposition."

I told him it was the easiest grand he'd ever make. All he had to do was toss the incendiary device of his choice into an old empty house and drive away. He wouldn't even have to get out of the car. It was that simple. Five hundred before, another five when the job was completed.

He took a hit off his joint and held it in till his eyes bugged out like a squashed bullfrog. Without exhaling he said, "Whose house am I torching?"

"Mine."

He coughed out a laugh. "What is this, some kinda insurance scam?"

I didn't say anything.

"Okay, none of my business. Less I know, the better, right?"

"You know the house, right?"

"Your house? Sure, I know your house. That crazy looking place down the street from the garage."

"So, what do you think? You interested?"

Barker picked something off the end of his tongue. "I might could be," he said. "That house sits on an alley, right? Along the railroad tracks?"

"There's another alley on the south side that's even more out of the way."

"Cool, two alleys." He held the joint up and studied the burn. "You say the house is empty?"

"Not even a rat. The ex-wife and kids moved out weeks ago."

Suddenly the music hiccoughed and made a slurred, slow-motion sound.

"Goddamn it! Fucking shit!" Barker punched the ejector with his finger and the tape popped out. He yanked on the cassette, but the tape had got itself wrapped around the guts of the machine. "Dammit, I just stole that fucking cassette!"

I sighed and rolled up the side window. My gaunt reflection stared back at me. I almost didn't recognize myself. I looked so old and haggard. It honestly freaked me out for a moment.

Barker pulled on the cassette till the tape snapped. Then he rolled down the window and tossed it angrily out into the snow.

"There goes five bucks."

"I thought you said you stole it?"

"So? What's your point?"

I let him stew another moment before I again asked him if he was interested. He took a last hit off the joint and tossed the roach out the window next to the ruined cassette.

"This house—you still own it?"

"Sure, me and the ex-wife. I mean, it's under contract, but that shouldn't matter."

He nodded and looked like he was thinking it over, though it was impossible to say what was going on inside that head. After a moment, he turned to me and said, "Okay, I'll do it for two grand."

I had been hoping I wouldn't have to go that high. That extra grand could have lasted me another two, three months. As long as I kept off the booze and didn't eat much—which I didn't, anyway.

On the other hand, good arsonists don't come cheap.

"Fifteen hundred," I said.

"Like I said, I'll do it for two grand."

"Fine," I said. "Half now and the other half when it's done."

"That's cool."

I nodded. "Wait here."

I went back to the station wagon and got another five hundred from the footlocker. I kept one eye on Barker. I trusted him about as much as I trusted a rattlesnake with a toothache. Then I went back to the Dodge and handed Barker the grand through the passenger side window.

"Buy yourself a new cassette," I said.

Barker scratched at his chin to hide a smile. Slowly, he counted the bills. I don't think he'd ever seen that much money at one time.

"How soon you want it done?"

"How soon do you want the other half?"

He winked at me. "In that case, I better get busy."

I leaned on the window frame and glanced around at the park, the backstops and metal bleachers, the cinderblock dugouts, the shuttered concession stands, the snow-covered ball fields. "Just let me know when you're gonna do it so I can plan to be somewhere with a lot of people."

Barker tapped the side of his head with the bills. "Alibi witnesses. That's using the old noodle."

He slipped the cash into his jacket pocket.

"You got a pen?" I said.

"A pen?"

"And something to write on. I want to give you my number."

"You want me to call you?"

"When you decide on a day and time."

"On the phone?"

I sighed heavily. "Use a phone booth if you don't trust your phone."

"How 'bout I just come over—?"

"No! Jesus! Do you have a pen or not?"

Barker shrugged and rooted round in his glove box—it was crammed full of stolen tools and drug paraphernalia—till he found a pencil nub and what looked like an old unpaid parking ticket.

I wrote down my mother's phone number and gave it back to him. "Destroy this after you call me."

Barker shrugged. "I wasn't gonna pay it, anyway."

"And don't freak if an old lady answers the phone. That's my mother."

"You live with your mother?"

I didn't say anything.

"That's cool. She got a nice place? You remember my place, don't ya? Used to belong to my grandma?"

I straightened. "Call when you decide when you're gonna do it."

Barker folded the scrap paper and shoved it into his jacket pocket next to the cash. "After this is over, you oughta come out to my place for some beers."

"After I pay you off, we're never going to see each other again."

Barker gave me a sad, confused look, like I'd just broken up with him. I tapped my good hand on the window frame and turned and walked back to the station wagon.

For two thousand bucks, he'd get over it all right.

EIGHT

BARKER CALLED early next morning. I assume from a phone booth. We were on for that evening. He couldn't tell me what time exactly, just that it would be between 8 p.m. and 1 a.m.

"You can't narrow it down a little more than that?"

"Hey man, I don't tell you how to do your job," he said. "Oh, that's right. You're *between* jobs."

"Fine. Eight to one is fine."

"Who was that?" my mother asked after I hung up. "Was that about a job?"

She had been up since 6 a.m., and since I slept on the pull-out sofa, I, too, had been up since 6 a.m. Watching television, of course. I tried to remember what she had done before she and the old man bought their first television set in the early sixties. Then I remembered. She smoked cigarettes and stared at the radio.

"It wasn't about a job."

"Of course not. I hope you don't think you're gonna loaf around my place all day like some charity case. And don't try and tell me there's no work. My daddy used to say a man with a truck never lacks for work, and that was during the Depression."

"I drive a station wagon."

"Excuses, that's what you got."

By seven-thirty in the morning, I'd had enough. I got dressed and left the apartment. I had no particular destination in mind. I couldn't go to a bar—which would have been the obvious choice—and it was too cold to wander the streets or sit in a park feeding ducks. So, I ended up hiding out in the public library, of all places. Normally a library is the last place on Earth you would find me. I never understood the point of building these big, grand buildings just to lend out books—not when they could be lending out something useful, like tools or kerosene heaters or winter coats. I mean, the bums go there to get warm. Why not just lend them a kerosene heater and a coat and they wouldn't have to go there and stink up the place? But then what do I know?

I cursed Greg the whole way to the library. You think because a guy's a millionaire, he knows things, but the fact is most guys get their wealth from their parents or by stealing it or a con game or figuring out how to game the system. You ask me, smarts have very little to do with it.

I found an empty table by the second-floor fire escape where I hoped I wouldn't be disturbed. I sat down and lay my head down on my arms. I knew it was a risk on account of the dreams I'd been having lately, the ones where I wake up screaming my fool head off. It used to scare the hell out of Sandy and the kids, no matter how many times it happened. I guess you never get used to your old man's terrified screams at three in the morning. They always seemed to get worse when I was stressed out, and boy, was I feeling stressed out now. I didn't think I'd be able to fall asleep, though. My mind was running ten miles a minute. For one thing, I still hadn't come up with an alibi. A rock-solid alibi would mean spending the evening with a bunch of people who knew me, and since I didn't have any real friends and I never belonged to any social clubs or joined a bowling league, and since an A.A. meeting only lasted an hour, tops, I didn't have a whole lot of options.

There was just no way around it. I was going to have to go to a bar.

And just like that, six months on the wagon... shot to hell.

On the bright side, six wasted months was a hell of a lot better than five to ten years for arson.

My regular bar was out. Chuck's was only a block from our house, and would put me right in the vicinity. That left my reserve bar, Tony's Tavern, and I sure couldn't sit at Tony's drinking Coca-Colas. The regulars would know something was screwy. Everything had to be as normal as breathing. When my house was a smoldering ash heap, I was going to be the main suspect. That meant the cops would swarm like insects all over Tony's, grilling the bar flies.

"Did you see Al Heidorn here last night?"

"Sure, I saw him. I remember he was acting kinda strange."

"How do you mean, strange?"

"He was drinking soda pop. Al never drank a soda pop in his life before last night."

"You don't say."

At the same time, I wanted to give the drunks something to remember me by. Something that wasn't suspicious, like drinking soda pop would be. I considered wearing a goofy hat or an ugly sweater.

"Sure. I saw Al. How can I forget? He was wearing this goofy hat and drinking soda pop. There was definitely something off about him that night."

What was I getting all uptight about? I hadn't been to Tony's in six months. They'd remember me, all right.

There was one more thing. Not a big deal, but when I showed up at my mother's apartment at one in the morning drunk as a boiled owl, ma was going to be pissed. She was liable to toss me out on my ear. Try to, anyway.

Dammit, I wasn't thinking straight. I should have kept that motel room for another night.

I wondered what else I wasn't seeing? I considered driving back to the motel, see if I couldn't get the key back, then I decided against it. I'd just have to pray Ma was a heavy sleeper and hope for the best.

I lay my head down on the table and within a few minutes, I'd drifted off to sleep.

Around two o'clock a homely, cross-eyed librarian awakened me. She told me I was screaming in my sleep and scaring the other patrons. She told me I had to leave. I wanted to tell her that her creepy ass was scaring the patrons, too, but I didn't because I'm too nice. So, I just got up and left.

I drove back to my mother's apartment. I told her I'd spent the day down at the job center filling out applications and skills assessment questionnaires and talking to staff, but they just didn't have a thing for me. I don't think she believed it, not for a minute, but she couldn't prove otherwise.

I hung around the apartment the next four hours as my mother chain-smoked Salems and stared at the TV. Poor ma, she was just running out the clock, waiting for the stage 4 lung cancer diagnoses that would inevitably put her out of her misery. Meanwhile, I killed time leafing through a stack of old photo albums, blurry black and white snapshots of me and my sister and my dead brother as kids on long ago birthdays and Christmas mornings, and faded Polaroids of the old man with a shit-eating grin on his face, holding up strings of fish he'd caught or standing in front of one or another of the many used cars we'd had. Always American cars. Pop had a thing for Buicks. All those spooky old photographs got me thinking about the family home and how it had been growing up there. We were poor as church mice, but so were most of the people in our part of town, so it wasn't a big deal. Somehow we found a way to get the things we needed even if they were second or third hand. We built our own bicycles out of discarded parts and when we turned sixteen, we learned how to make abandoned junk cars run better than ever. We didn't play sports or play in bands like the rich and middle-class kids. We got jobs carrying the newspaper or doing yard work or taking out the trash or breaking down cardboard beer boxes at Chuck Inn back, when Chuck was still alive and would pay you a nickel per box.

I turned a page and came upon a faded snapshot of my parents, all dressed up and standing in front of the house. Some big occasion, I guess. I took the photo out of its plastic sleeve and studied it closely. They looked like they were in their mid-twenties. I was probably fifteen years older now than the old man was in that photograph. He had another thirty years to go before his ticker up and quit on him. He gave the camera a drunken smile; ma wore her customary scowl. She was holding a baby. My dead brother Leroy. The old man held a brown bottle of beer.

I slipped the photo into my jacket pocket.

I GOT TO Tony's around seven. Tony's catered to a sportsy clientele, bowlers and fast-pitch softball players, while Chuck's was more the sullen, crying-in-your-beer crowd. My kind of people.

I glanced around the bar in bewilderment. I didn't know a soul in the place; even the lady bartender was new. A couple of shaggy headed kids leaned on the bar and stared at a hockey game on the TV, and off in the corner sat an old, emaciated smoker with a bad case of the shakes who I vaguely recalled seeing once or twice before. I couldn't remember his name, but his hacking cough and long, creepy yellow fingernails seemed familiar. I gave a friendly nod to the old coot and pulled up beside him. He struck me as the somber, slightly eccentric type. An old wino like him wouldn't be much of an alibi. What I needed was someone half coherent who could place me at the bar from roughly seven to midnight. Someone who could remain sober enough to remember seeing me. The only one who fit the bill was the bartender.

She drifted over, and I turned on my best smile, the one where I avoid showing my bad teeth. Christ, it had been so long since I'd smiled I thought I'd break my face. She was a big-boned, curvy thing, mid-thirties, heavy on the war paint and hairspray. Not fat, necessarily, though she probably had a good thirty pounds on me. Just middle aged and heavy enough that the guys weren't constantly hitting on her. I checked out her digits. No ring.

I ordered my first beer in almost six months. The Budweiser tasted just like I remembered. Like stale horse piss. I nursed the draft and tried to work up the nerve to talk to the bartender. She didn't look like the kind of gal that got a lot of passes. When she had her back to me, I slipped off my ring; I'd forgotten I was still wearing the damn thing. What do divorced guys do with their old wedding bands, anyway? The one I had wasn't even real gold. Gold-plated, maybe. Not even worth pawning. I slipped the ring in my pocket and hoped she hadn't noticed.

It was probably a good thing she was new. She had no way of knowing I was a divorced, unemployed recovering alcoholic who was about to belly flop off the wagon—and there was nobody in the bar to put her wise. Anyway, I wasn't looking to screw her. I just needed an alibi. Although she wasn't bad looking, in her sad, pitiful little way, and it *had* been a while...

I pulled up an ashtray and lit a smoke. Next to me, the old guy coughed and the hockey fans cheered as a fight erupted on the ice. Presently, the bartender sauntered down to my end of the bar and ran a damp rag over the mahogany and asked the old coot if he was ready for another. He nodded grimly.

I was feeling extra jumpy tonight. On top of everything else, I hadn't flirted with a woman since I started dating Sandy. I was twenty-three years out of practice.

She brought the old guy's drink and asked me if I was ready for another. I couldn't think of anything clever to say, so I just nodded my head. By the time she returned with the mug, I had resolved to introduce myself. It turned out her name was Roxy, and it was only her second week on the job. She said she liked it all right.

"Haven't seen you before," she said. "First time in?"

"Me? No, but I've been away awhile." That was no good. That sounded like I'd been in the joint, so I quickly added that I'd been working down in Texas the past six months and had just got back into town.

"I love Texas," she said dreamily. "I got a sister lives in north Dallas."

"I was right near there. Centerton."

Her eyes brightened. "I know Centerton. It's lovely."

That was not exactly how I would describe it, but okay, whatever.

Suddenly, Roxy arched an eyebrow at me. "Did you lose something?"

"How's that?"

"Weren't you wearing a gold ring when you sat down?"

I gave her a closed-mouth grin. "You're pretty observant, Roxy."

"Women notice little things like that."

I knew all about women noticing things, so I laughed good-naturedly. "I'm recently divorced. It was burning my finger, anyway."

I took the ring out of my pocket and tapped it nervously on the bar. "I was just wondering, what do folks do with these things after a divorce?"

Roxy shrugged. "Do I look like a divorcee?"

I laughed again. "That was a… what-you-call-it…"

"Rhetorical question," said the old coot at the end of the bar. I gave him a look that said, *Who the hell asked you to butt in?*

"I pawned mine," Roxy said. "My engagement ring, I mean. Got three hundred dollars for it. The wedding ring wasn't worth much. I think I got twenty for that. Whatever it was, it sure wasn't worth all the grief."

She looked at me and smiled a little sadly. Then she picked up her rag and went down to the far end of the bar. I got a good look at her big ass in those tight white jeans. I tried to imagine what it might be like, me and her, but it only depressed me. Two in the morning and stumbling back to her pitiful little apartment with the sad clown prints on the walls and the peacock feathers in big blue vases, and her kids, teenage girls, still up, whining about being grounded or missing their periods.

Anyway, I had other things on my mind. My gaze shifted to the Clydesdale clock over the bar. 7:45. Bar time, so it was more like 7:30.

I went into my shirt pocket for my cigarettes and found the old black and white snapshot of my parents and Leroy. I studied the photo in the bar light. A real portrait of loss. The old man was gone. Leroy was gone. Ma was nearly gone. In a few hours, the house would be gone—along with my two thousand bucks.

Suddenly, I was having doubts. Cold feet. Was it worth it, all that cash, not to mention the risk of getting caught and doing hard time? And for what? Family pride? Why the hell should I be proud of my family? A long line of ditch diggers, drop-outs and drunkards. Or just for a chance to stick it to my ex? It wasn't too late to call the whole thing off. I studied the phone behind the bar. All it would take was one call to Barker. Okay, so calling Barker on the phone probably wasn't an option. I'd have to drive to my house and wait for him, hopefully catch him before he burned the place down.

"What's that?" Roxy stood over me, her big jugs resting on the bar for my benefit.

I slipped the photograph into my pocket and hemmed and hawed. I sure as shit couldn't show her a snapshot of a house that might well be a crime scene at this very moment.

"It's... uh... nothing." I left it at that.

"Nothing?"

"Yeah. Really."

I smiled. She gave me a quizzical look, then she shrugged and went off to get one of the hockey fans a bottle of beer.

What the hell was wrong with me? Call it off? I must be getting soft. Hell no, I wasn't going to call it off. I got up off the stool and went over to the jukebox. I looked for "Baby Let's Play House." I wanted to hear Elvis sing that line that went, "I'd rather see you dead little girl than see you with another man."

They didn't have it, so I played "Suspicious Minds" instead. But it wasn't the same.

It was now 7:55. I ordered another draft, listened to the old coot laughing to himself, and I watched some of the hockey game. I couldn't have cared less about the game, but it was a way to kill time.

Another hour dragged by and still no familiar faces. I was getting more and more anxious, afraid my whole alibi was going to depend on this one broad, when the back door opened and a short, pale, redheaded guy entered. Carl Porterfield. At last, a familiar face. I couldn't stand the bastard, but he'd just become my new best friend. Carl Porterfield was a fairly successful realtor in town, a renowned backslapper and a fanatic when it came to golf. It was all the guy could talk about. I couldn't think of a single thing more boring than golf—except maybe talking about golf, but tonight I was going to talk golf if it killed me.

I nodded to Carl. "Hey Carl. Play any golf lately?"

He grinned and sauntered down to my end of the bar. We pumped and squeezed the hell out of each other's hands.

"Little too much snow on the ground the past couple of days," he said, "but I did manage to get in eighteen over at Tamarack Saturday before the storm hit." And he was off, shattering the record for world's biggest bore.

I lit a cigarette and nodded like a drooling idiot. I didn't hear a word of it, but managed to grunt and nod at all the right places. When he was all talked out, I steered the conversation to the televised hockey game—who was playing and who was ahead and who scored how many for which team. When the cops came nosing around, I wanted Carl to know the score—literally.

"Sure Al Heidorn was in. That was the night the Blues got hammered by the Canucks, five to one. Unger just managed to slip one past Kermit with a minute twenty left on the clock.

They played like a bunch of headless chickens."

Suddenly Carl finished his drink, got to his feet, and said he had to hit the road. What the hell, I thought, the guy had come in for one drink? Nobody ever came into Tony's for one drink!

I could feel the panic deep in my bowels and I seized Carl by the arm and asked him what's the rush? He looked at my hand on his arm, and it wasn't a friendly look either, so I turned him loose. I told him I was celebrating my divorce and he should have one on me, anything he wanted, top shelf stuff, but the bastard demurred, said the wife was expecting him. I brought up golf again, asked if he had played the new course up in East Alton, but he had already started paying for his drink. I watched him walk out the door and when I glanced up at the clock. It was only 8:30.

I looked around at all the empty tables. It was Friday night, for chrissake. Where the hell was everybody?

The old coot hacked and gave me a wink. "Divorce party, eh?"

I didn't say anything. I flagged down Roxy and asked her what time the joint would start to pick up and she shrugged and said, nine thirty, ten o'clock, depending on the weather.

The weather didn't look too bad. Damn cold, but it didn't look like snow.

I'd about had it with draft beer. I needed something to make the time pass quicker. I had Roxy pour me a Jim Beam on the rocks. It wasn't long before the bourbon kicked in. *Welcome back, old friend. How I've missed you!* After that, it was easy to talk to Roxy. But when a bowling team came in—more guys I didn't know—I might as well have been the invisible man.

Some time later, when I staggered back from the men's room, I noticed the place had begun to pick up. A dozen more people had drifted in; one of them, an attractive young gal, looked familiar. I couldn't remember her name—I never remember names—but I was almost sure she had been friends with my oldest daughter. Maybe not friends, but certainly classmates. She was with another gal I didn't recognize. What they were doing in a middle-aged guy bar, I do not know. Slumming? A dare? Whatever the reason, I knew they wouldn't stay long. Not once they got a good look at the clientele and some of the pathetic old men started hitting on them.

I had just lit up a smoke when I felt a tap on my shoulder.

"Hey Mr. Heidorn. Remember me?"

I turned and flashed my daughter's classmate a drunken, tight-lipped smile. She looked even better up close, and her friend was finer still. "Sure, I do," I said. "You're Rose's friend."

She gave me a kittenish look, like she wanted to play. "Yeah, what's my name?"

"Oh, hell..."

Both girls giggled. "I'm Kate and this is Jolene."

"I knew that, and none of this mister crap. Call me Al." I leaned in close and got a whiff of Kate's perfume. She smelled like all the flowers of Eden after a fresh spring rain. "Say, are you two old enough to be in here?"

They giggled again, and the one called Jolene asked after Rosie.

"Who?"

"Rose! Your daughter!"

"Oh, Rose," I said. "Fine. She's doing real fine." The fact was, I had no idea how Rose was doing. She could've been in San Quentin for all I knew. Like I said, she wouldn't give me or her mother her phone number. We weren't even sure what town she was living in.

"She still working at the bank?"

"Just got a big promotion," I lied.

"Good for her!"

Talk about a pair of knockout alibis! If only I could figure a way to keep them from leaving. Of course, that would mean keeping them entertained for a couple of hours. That would be a good trick, seeing as how I had very little cash, no sense of humor, and all the charm of a hangman. Not to mention I was old enough to be their fathers.

"Lemme buy you girls some drinks." I spun around toward the bar—too fast, it turned out. I nearly toppled off the stool. Christ, how drunk was I? I told myself to slow down a little so I could remember things, in case I was grilled about it later. Saying, "How the hell do I know, I was falling-down drunk?" wouldn't help my case much.

Seeing me talking to those young chicks seemed to have gotten Roxy's attention. She came over to check on me and give the girls the stink eye. Being six months out of practice, I was hoping to take things slowly, but nope, the girls wanted to do tequila shots and what was I going to do, say no?

Besides slamming tequila shots, I had no idea how to keep a couple of twenty-year-old girls entertained at a bar. The pool table was occupied. I tried to remember some dirty jokes, but I've always had a lousy memory for jokes. About the only things I can't forget are all the stupid things I've said and done. One of the girls asked me about my hand and I gave them a long, dramatic story about fending off a mugger with a knife. That piqued their interest—for a while, at least. Then I got the brilliant idea to tell them I was celebrating my divorce, celebrating being a free man again, and we drank more shots to that. The liquor hit me all at once and the next thing I knew, I was talking real loud about how I was ready to party all night long and we should all go dancing somewhere, then I felt something rumble in my stomach. I made a mad, drunken dash to the back door and out to the parking lot. I slipped on a patch of ice and went down hard, landing on my bad hand. Then I vomited about a gallon of booze.

I thought I'd just lie there in a puddle of puke for a while. It seemed like the best option.

I expected the girls to be gone when I finally got back, but I was wrong again. I guess they were enjoying the free drinks and the drunken antics of a pathetic, divorced, middle-aged man.

The next hour passed in a blur. Roxy had turned off the sound on the hockey game and turned up the jukebox and I have a vague and horrible recollection of me and the girls singing loudly and drunkenly to *Stayin' Alive,* even though I don't know any of the words. I counted three dozen people in the bar, but it's possible I was seeing double. The next thing I knew, Roxy was leaning her big jugs across the counter and yelling over the music: "Phone call! Says his name's Mike Barker!"

Jesus Christ! I thought. *Why doesn't he just rent a billboard?*

I got up from the stool, took a moment to steady myself, then reeled around to the side of the bar. Roxy laid her bedroom eyes on me and handed me the phone.

"What are you doing, giving her your name?" I hissed into the phone.

"Al?"

"Of all the stupid..." I took a deep breath. "So... How'd it go?"

"Mission accomplished."

I glanced at the Clydesdale clock. It was quarter past eleven. "Any problems?"

"Problems? Like what?"

I lowered my voice. "How should I know? Did anybody see you? Did you leave any prints anywhere?"

He laughed. "You think I'm that stupid?"

It was hard to hear over the high-pitched harmonies and the bowlers braying like drunken jackasses. God, I couldn't wait to get the hell out of there, back to my quiet, dreary old bar where the drunks knew how to behave themselves.

"So, when do I get the other grand?"

"Tomorrow. You get it tomorrow."

We made arrangements to meet at the park at dusk. After I hung up, I stepped outside and stood alone in the parking lot, breathing in deep lungfuls of icy air. Now that it was over, I thought I might feel something. I'm not sure what—a sense of retribution... satisfaction... vindication, one of them twenty-five-cent words. But I didn't feel much of anything except plastered. And tired. I fired up a Marlboro and then I heard something.

About eight blocks north, a couple of sirens commenced to wail. It was too dark to see any billowing clouds of smoke. I leaned against a telephone pole and finished the smoke. Then I went back inside.

I couldn't believe Rose's friends were still hanging around. What the hell was wrong with them?

Kate gave me a curious look. "You know Mike Barker?"

My heart knocked. "Um. What?"

"Weren't you just talking to him on the phone?"

For chrissake, how did these two nice, attractive girls know Mike Barker?

Sure, it was a small town, but it wasn't that small.

So now my alibis knew Barker had called me five minutes after my house went up in flames. I could have killed that stupid son of a bitch.

Jolene said, "I went to school with him, seventh and eighth grade. I think he'd been held back a few years."

"I didn't know you went to reform school," Kate said, and followed this up with a drunken laugh.

"You're so funny," Jolene said. "He was such a little creep. They used to tell all kinds of stories about him. How he'd bury cats up to their necks and run 'em over with a lawnmower."

"Oh my god! I'm gonna be sick!" Kate said, paling visibly. "Didn't he, like, almost kill some old guy a few years ago? Wasn't it in the paper? He beat some old man half to death with a tire iron after he got cut off in traffic?"

"Wouldn't surprise me," Jolene said. "Why isn't that psychopath in jail?"

I swallowed the last of my drink and said, "Parker. I was talking to a Mike Parker."

"Oh," Kate said. "I thought she said Barker."

"So did I," Jolene said.

"Yeah, no, different guy."

I wasn't sure if they believed me or not. What I did know was after that, my mood soured considerably. They were useless as alibis now, since there was a chance they'd mention Barker to the cops.

I'd wasted all that time and money for nothing.

The girls must have noticed my sudden mood swing. They said they were going to go some place to dance. That was fine by me.

We said goodbye, and I glanced at the Clydesdales. It was almost eleven thirty. I looked over at Roxy, who was busy laughing it up with a couple of bowlers. There were now a few guys I knew in the bar and I made a point of stopping and saying hello on my way to the men's room, even though they wouldn't be able to do me a whole lot of good at this point. I wanted to punch a hole in the bathroom wall, but my hand was still hurting like hell from that spill in the parking lot, and the thought of punching with my left hand didn't give me as much satisfaction.

I stepped outside to get some air and clear my head a bit. I still needed to hang around for at least another hour. It was too cold to stand around outside, so I went back in the bar and started drinking Roxy's stale coffee, trying to sober up enough to drive home without killing anyone. The whole point of this night was to stay *out* of jail.

I was left alone the rest of the night. Even Roxy ignored me. Around 1 a.m., I paid the small fortune that was my tab and got in my station wagon and drove carefully and uneventfully to my mother's apartment. I quietly let myself, keeping the lights off. In the dark, unfamiliar room, I immediately banged my shins, tripped, fell, got up and banged my shins again.

Ma was in her bedroom, the door closed. She had put out a pillow and a sheet for me. No blanket. I guess she was hoping I would freeze to death. I sat down on the couch and started to untie my shoes.

Her door opened. "Look at you," she cried. "You're drunk. I could smell you all the way in my room with the door closed. Drying out my ass. I should have known better than to trust you. Now you get the hell out of my apartment."

I removed one shoe and started in on the other lace. "It's one thirty in the morning, Ma. Where am I supposed to go?"

"That's not my problem," she said. "Now get out!"

I fell over on the couch. "I'll leave in the morning. Right now, I'm going to sleep."

Ma carried on, ranting and raving some more, but it didn't bother me in the least. I was out cold.

NINE

"WHO'S KNOCKING AT my door at this hour?"

A light went on. Or maybe a star exploded. I shaded my eyes with my hand and slowly raised up on my elbow. It took a moment for things to come together. I was on a couch. My mother's couch. I glanced at my watch. It was a little after 3 a.m. A massive bomb seemed to have gone off inside my skull. No one could have survived such a blast. I had been immune to hangovers before I stopped drinking. There's a lesson there.

"Don't answer it," I said thickly. Nothing good ever came from answering your door at 3 a.m.

Ma opened the door. "Dear God, Albert James, what have you done now?"

A large, bald cop stood there.

"Detective Hill, Belleville Police," he said. "I'm looking for Al Heidorn."

Ma turned to me. "You haven't been in my house two nights, and already you've brought the law here."

The detective nodded toward me. "Mr. Heidorn?"

My mother frowned and said, "I hope you got a warrant."

I was dressed in soiled boxers and a ragged T-shirt, my clothes bunched on the floor at my feet. He had either come by to tell me that my house burned down, or he was there to arrest me. In which case, somebody must have seen Barker. Got his license plate number. And the cops, they must have picked him up and worked him over. And not long after that, the son of a bitch ratted me out.

I wondered how many years a man could get for burning down his own house.

Ma glared at the detective. "Well?"

"Ma'am?" he said.

"The warrant?"

"I don't need to come in, Ma'am, I'd just like to speak to your son," he said. The detective craned his neck to get a look at me. "Are you Al Heidorn?"

Ma folded her arms and leaned against the doorjamb. "You don't have to answer that," she said. "Make him get a warrant." She turned and narrowed her eyes on me and asked the cop, "What did he do? *Allegedly*."

"We had a heck of a time tracking you down," the detective said to me. Then he gestured toward the hallway. "Mind if we speak in private?"

The cop sure wasn't acting like he was arresting an arsonist. Calling me mister, asking if I mind stepping outside. Maybe he didn't want to upset my mother more than she already was. Maybe he suspected she was a bit unstable. Or maybe Barker hadn't managed to screw things up after all.

Ma's eyes shifted from me to the detective. "One of you may as well tell me what this is about. I'm gonna find out sooner or later."

"Yes, ma'am," the detective said. "I just need to speak to your son alone for a minute."

She muttered under her breath and stepped away from the door. I sat up on the couch. It hurt to move—every movement sent a nerve signal that was like a rubber mallet to the head. But I got to my feet and struggled into my jeans and flannel shirt. I couldn't find my boots anywhere. Could I have lost them somewhere, driven home barefoot? As messed up as I was, anything could have happened.

"Am I gonna need shoes?"

He nodded. "And a jacket."

A bad sign. Maybe I *was* going to be arrested.

I found my boots under the couch and asked the detective to hang on while I emptied my bladder. I staggered into the bathroom and leaned over the toilet. I felt like I was going to vomit, but it was a false alarm. I took a long piss and found a bottle of aspirin in the medicine cabinet and swallowed four of them with a big gulp of water from the tap. Making a run for it wasn't even a consideration. Ma was on the third floor and the apartment had only the one door. I grabbed my jacket and closed the door. We walked down the hall a bit, far enough so ma couldn't hear us. I had to remind myself to act surprised and angry when he broke the news about the fire.

"Do you own a house at Three South 19th Street?"

I looked him squarely in the eyes. "Why do you ask?"

The detective frowned. "How about you answer the question?"

"I guess so. I mean… Are you gonna tell me what this is about?"

"Were you aware that there was a fire at that address last night?"

"Fire? What kind of fire?"

"A bad one."

"Three South 19th?"

"That's correct."

"The house was empty. What happened?"

"Actually—"

"Do they know how it started?"

"We're not sure yet. There'll be an investigation. But there's something else."

I steeled myself.

"There was a fatality."

"A what—?"

"A fatality. A boy. A teenager."

The words hit me like a bucket of ice water. I stiffened and felt the back of my legs go weak.

It wasn't possible.

"You okay, Mr. Heidorn?"

I leaned my back against the wall. "You said a boy?"

The detective nodded.

"A teenage boy?"

"That's correct."

I forced myself to breathe. "Who…?"

"We're not sure yet. That's why we'd like you to come with us. We'd like to see if you can identify the body."

"Why me?"

"It was your house."

He talked on for a while, but I could make out very little of what he was saying over the storm thrashing around in my skull. It wasn't possible. It had to be some other kid. Some random teen. A runaway or something. Frank was safe and sound… Somewhere. With those twins, those friends of his. Sure. That's it.

"What did the boy look like?" I said.

The detective nodded toward the stairs. "We can talk about it on the way."

ONLY WE DIDN'T talk about it. We drove in silence, the only sound the occasional squawk of the police radio. Five minutes later, we pulled up to the back doors of the Catholic hospital. By then, my mind had stopped working, and I had completely shut down. I stared blankly out the window of the patrol car. Big mounds of dirty snow piled on the empty hospital parking lot. Some staticky chatter came across the police band.

I wasn't sure of my voice, but I swallowed hard and said, "Where did you find him?"

"Fire department found him. I believe he was in the basement."

Frank slept in an old coal bunker in the rear of the basement that I'd fixed up as a storage room. It was dry and had a small window where the coal used to come in, and one day he just moved in there without asking. What was I going to do—a boy needs his privacy.

"How did... how did it happen?"

"We won't know the official cause of death till the autopsy, but in these cases, it's almost always smoke inhalation."

It got quiet in the car.

"And you don't know how it started?"

"That's under investigation."

The officer picked up his clipboard and eased out of the patrol car. I followed in a daze. He pressed a bell, and the door buzzed and clicked open. We walked down a long basement hallway, which led to another door. He pressed another bell and again we were buzzed in.

We stood in a small white room with a small desk piled with registers and other such books. On one side, there was what looked like a walk-in cooler, like you find in taverns. An old man in a frayed lab coat and round eyeglasses with wild tufts of hair over his ears strode in. He shook hands with the detective. They made some small talk about the weather, then the old man opened the door to the cooler.

Inside were three gray body bags stretched out on stainless steel carts. The old man checked the tags, then rolled out one of the carts. The three of us stood there staring at the bag, waiting for something to happen.

The old man turned to me and lifted his eyebrows. "Okay?"

I didn't feel like it was okay at all. I still felt like the police or the fire department or someone had made some terrible mistake, and that I shouldn't even be there.

Maybe I should just go, I thought.

"Mr. Heidorn?" the detective said.

I took a deep breath and nodded. I forced myself to look as he unzipped the bag.

I took a step back as the wind rushed out of my lungs. My

insides iced over. I couldn't breathe. I was dying. I squeezed my eyes shut as hot tears leaked down my cheeks, so hot they burned my skin.

"Can you identify this boy?" the old man said.

He didn't look dead. He didn't look asleep either. He needed a haircut.

"Mr. Heidorn, is this your son?" the detective said.

I turned my face away. I may have nodded my head.

I heard the zipper going up and the sound of the cart rumble back into the cooler.

They went on doing things, their jobs, going down the checklist of things to do after a body's been identified. It was just another day at the office.

After a while, I turned and walked out into the hallway. A moment later, the detective came up beside me and offered me the standard condolences. Then he handed me a clipboard to sign and said, "We'd like you to come down to the station."

TEN

THEY PUT ME IN a small, drab room in the basement of the police station. Detective Hill stood in the doorway saying things, but I didn't hear a word of it. I was listening to my own thoughts, which were like a dozen madmen bouncing around in my skull screaming all at once, telling me what a lousy son of a bitch I was.

"Al?"

I looked at him.

"Can I get you something? Water or coffee?"

I couldn't speak. I shook my head. It seemed like the end. You know when you've reached the end... There's nothing there... You're there, but you don't exist. It's just nothingness, where nothing matters... Whether you live or die. Whether you confess or don't confess.

The detective nodded toward a chair and said, "Have a seat."

I pulled out the chair closest to the door, and the detective shook his head. "Not that one. Over there."

I wasn't feeling drunk anymore. Just stunned. I moved around to the far side of the table and sat down. I tried to say something, but it was like the words were all gummed up in my throat.

The detective strode over to a file cabinet and started opening drawers, peering inside, and slamming them shut. Whatever he was looking for didn't seem to be there.

All I could think was if I ever got out of that place, I was going to crawl up inside a bottle and never come out. I ran my hand over my stubbly chin and said, "Does my wife—ex-wife know?"

The detective rifled through the bottom drawer, then slammed it closed. He looked up. "We haven't been able to locate her yet. You got any idea where we might find her?"

I shook my head. They found me. They could find her.

But then something turned around in me. Just thinking about Sandy made the blood pump in my throat. Sandy and Russ. They were the reason Frank had been in that house in the first place. That was no accident. And the house sale. The divorce... They had all been her idea. Moving in with that rotten son of bitch.

And Barker. Why hadn't he checked to make sure the house was empty? You always check. There could be squatters in there. Or kids drinking and screwing inside. You always check.

Detective Hill said he'd be right back and stepped out into the hall. I heard a click as a deadbolt slid into place. From the sound of it, I wasn't going anywhere. I wondered how much they knew. They must have known something, or they wouldn't have locked me in.

I got up and took off my jacket, and draped it over the back of the chair. Alone now, I tried to gather my thoughts. I wasn't so sure I wanted to make a statement after all. I mean, I could think of at least three people who were as guilty as I was—if not more so.

I must have set a new record, the way I went from suicidal to homicidal in a matter of seconds. I had to figure a way to turn this thing around, or at least put the brakes on. It hadn't occurred to me I might need a lawyer, but it did now. If I didn't lawyer up, I'd have to answer their questions, and these detectives, they got ways to trip you up and I couldn't afford to get tripped up when my mind wasn't working right. God knows what they might trick me into saying.

Then again, asking for a lawyer would make me look like I had something to hide, and I was trying not to look that way. Being angry didn't make any sense either. A guy who'd just lost his only son is supposed to be devastated, not pissed off.

The detective returned with an old tape recorder; he set it down on the table in front of me. The machine looked like they had brought it out of retirement just for this occasion. He plugged a small microphone into the jack and said, "I'm gonna record our conversation, if that's okay with you, Al?"

I let a moment pass while I thought it over. Then I decided it was time I got some answers myself.

"What's going on here, officer?"

"Detective."

"Am I under arrest or something?"

The detective fixed his eyes on me. "Why would you be under arrest, Al?"

"I mean the recorder."

"We use them all the time," he said. "We're just trying to figure out what happened to your son… and your house. You want to know what happened, don't you?"

"You said there was a fire."

"Right, but what started the fire?"

"How would I know?"

"Well, you know the house. You'd know if there was any faulty wiring or gas leaks or what have you."

I shook my head. "I never had any problems with the gas or wiring."

"So, I can record?"

"I don't… What if I say no?"

"Then I'll just have to write everything down, which will take twice as long. You don't want to spend all night here, do you, Al?"

"Actually…" I was about to say I wanted to talk to a lawyer, but for some reason, I didn't. I held back.

"Yeah?" he said.

"Forget it," I said. "Go ahead."

He pressed the record and play buttons and held the cheap little microphone to his lips and spoke his name into the mic. Then he said, "Interview with Albert Heidorn" and gave the date and time. He pressed rewind and played it back and he seemed satisfied with it, then he pressed play and record again and set the microphone on a little plastic stand.

He asked me when I last saw my son.

"A few minutes ago," I said. "At the morgue."

"I'm sorry. I mean alive."

"Well, that would've been, I don't know, six, seven months ago. Before I moved to Texas."

"And you haven't seen him since you've been back in town?"

"No, like I said—"

"Why'd you move to Texas?"

"Why?"

"Yes, why?"

I shrugged. "To get away."

Why did I say that? I sounded guilty, like I was running away from something. Something bad. You see, this is why they tell you to get a lawyer and keep your big trap shut, whether you're guilty or not.

"Get away from what?"

"You know. This life. This town. Everything. You name it."

"That's a lot to get away from."

I gave a half shrug.

"So, what's wrong with this town?"

"Nothing."

I didn't really want to get into it. I mean, where would you even begin?

"I just wanted a fresh start," I said.

The detective nodded. "So you were gone for how long?"

"Like I said, about six months."

"Six months. Why'd you come back?"

I sat up in my chair. "I'm sorry, but I don't see what this has to do with... You said you wanted to know what happened to my son. What's any of this got to do with that? I don't see the connection."

The detective gave me a blank look. "You know how most cases are solved, Al?"

"Dumb luck?"

"By talking to people, by asking questions. There's ballistics, forensics, there's eyewitnesses, there's tips, there's confessions, but most of all it's talking to people. I'm going to be talking to a lot of people, but I figured I'd start with you, the homeowner, the father of the deceased. You see what I'm saying here? It's standard procedure, that's all. Nothing personal."

I looked at him, saying nothing.

"So what do you say? You want to tell me why you came back?"

I hunched over the table, my hands folded nervously in my lap. Sweat stood out on my forehead and my armpits went slick. "I couldn't find a job down there—not a good job, anyway—and I missed my kids."

He nodded. "You got how many kids?"

"Three. Two... Now," I said. "One's married and moved away."

He studied me. "What line of work are you in, Al?"

"I'm a grease monkey. Foreign cars, mostly."

"Texas is a big place. You couldn't find work in some garage down there?"

I shook my head. "I mean, yeah, I found shit work, laying carpet."

"How's that?"

"I had a job laying carpet. You ever lay carpet?"

"Any idea why—"

"Try doing it eight, nine hours a day, five days a week."

"Mm."

"It's no picnic."

"Uh-huh." The detective leaned back in his chair and adjusted something in his pants. "Any idea why your son was in that empty house?"

I shook my head again. "He was supposed to be with his mother."

"So why wasn't he?"

I shrugged. "Ask her."

"So you and..."

"Sandy."

"...Sandy are divorced?"

"Uh-huh."

"And you live with *your* mother?"

"I... temporarily."

"On her couch."

I didn't say anything.

"About last night..."

"Yeah?"

"You really tied one on, didn't you?"

"I guess I had a few."

The detective lifted his eyebrows. "A few dozen?"

I stared at the detective.

"Did you go any place in particular?"

"Tony's."

"The sports bar? You a big sports fan, Al?"

I shrugged. "Same as the next guy."

"They played terrible last night."

"Yeah."

"Like a bunch of bums."

The detective studied me. He must have thought I was a complete idiot. This was no ordinary interview with a grieving father. The bastard was grilling me, trying to get me to say something incriminating, hoping I'd slip up. They must have at least suspected arson, otherwise he wouldn't have been grilling me like he was.

And I still hadn't asked for a lawyer.

The detective leaned forward and folded his hands before his mouth. After a moment, he said, "I'm curious about your house. I saw it had a sale pending sign in front."

"Under contract."

He grinned slightly, almost imperceptibly. When I realized why, I wanted to kick myself.

"So you've been by the house?"

"I drove past."

"When was this?"

"Soon as I got back into town. I wanted to see the kids. I thought they were still living there."

"I don't understand. You didn't know where your kids were living?"

This cop was starting to get on my last nerve. Who the hell did he think he was, judging me? What did he know about me or my situation?

"I didn't know they'd moved in with my cousin," I said.

"So your wife's living with your cousin? I thought you didn't know where she was?"

"I—"

He gave me a look. "I was hoping you'd be honest with me, Al."

"It ain't that," I said, groping for a way out. "I wanted to tell her myself... about our son. I didn't want some stranger, some cop breaking the news. Better if it comes from me."

The detective stared. At length, he said, "This cousin—what's his name?"

"Russ. Russell Cole."

"You and Russell on good terms?"

"I haven't seen or talked to him in years."

"Okay, but last time you saw him, were you on good terms?"

"Last time I saw him, we were."

"But not now?"

I bet a lawyer would have said, "I advise you not to answer that." But I couldn't shut my mouth. "You mean because he's living with my wife… ex-wife? My kids?"

He nodded.

"I don't know what the terms are now."

"Okay, Al. Just one or two more questions."

I braced myself. So far, his questions hadn't been too bad. At least I don't think I'd said anything that would send me to the chair. Then again, what I knew about the law would fit on a postage stamp. Double spaced.

The detective said, "You know the first thing that jumps out at me when I look at this case? The fact your house burns down three days after you get back into town… after you've been gone more than six months. That's quite the coincidence, wouldn't you say?"

"I wouldn't call it a coincidence."

"What would you call it, then?"

"A goddamn tragedy," I said, getting my dander up. "Look, I'm no detective, but it ain't hard to figure out what happened. My son was staying there because my cousin drove him out of his house. My daughter told me Frank and the old man were going at it like cats and dogs." I paused and looked squarely at the detective. "Frank probably had some kind of heater down there with him, trying to keep from freezing to death. He must've kicked it over in his sleep, or a blanket got too close. There was one of them Coleman heaters in the basement. I'll tell you something else. You ought to be investigating my ex-wife for child neglect."

The detective sat quietly for a moment, then he said, "The fire didn't start in the basement. It was contained to the main floor."

I didn't know what to say to that. It didn't matter, anyway. It was only a matter of time before they stumbled on the shards of Barker's Molotov cocktail. It wasn't like we'd tried to hide the fact that it was arson.

The detective said, "What time did you go to Tony's last night."

I pretended to think about that. "Around seven. Left around one."

"Anybody see you there?"

"I don't know, the bartender, I guess. I think her name was Roxy."

"Anyone else?"

I gave a shrug and pretended to think it over some more. "I spoke to Carl Porterfield for a while. But he was only in for a half hour or so. There were a few others I said hi to. Bob Detterman. Tom May."

My alibi, I realized, was shit. It all depended on the bartender, and here I'd gone and snubbed her for my daughter's friends. I didn't mention Kate and the other girl. I couldn't remember the other girl's name, and I didn't want the cops talking to them and one of them letting slip that I had been on the phone with Mike Barker—or a Mike Parker—just minutes after my house burned to the ground.

Bad enough, the bartender had gotten Barker's name—though it hadn't appeared to mean anything to her.

The detective asked about homeowner's insurance and I told him we didn't have any. He said he would check into that, then he asked if I knew anyone who might have a grudge against me—me or my ex-wife, if we had any enemies.

It was a chance to throw some of the suspicion off me, but damned if I could think of anyone. I didn't have any friends or enemies. Not really. Then, all the sudden, I thought of that black kid that had been trying to get in my daughter's pants.

"There is this one kid," I said. "A black boy."

The detective looked up and fixed me with two tired, bloodshot eyes. "A black boy, you say?"

I knew what he was thinking. There were maybe three black kids in the whole town, and they got blamed for everything.

"What's this boy's name?"

"Eddie Grady."

He nodded slightly.

"You know him?"

"I think so," he said. "Tell me something. What would a kid

like that have against you?"

"He lived down the street from us. He used to come over and hang out, trying to get in my thirteen-year-old girl's pants. I told him to quit coming around—or else."

"Or else what?"

"That's it. Or else."

We shared a look at this, then the detective said, "You think that might've angered him enough to burn down your house?"

I gave him a shrug. "I don't know. You asked if anyone might've had a grudge against me, so I'm telling you. After I chased him off, he told me he was gonna get even."

At that, the detective gave me a pair of raised eyebrows. "He said those exact words? 'I'm gonna get even?'"

"Pretty much."

"Okay," he said, and turned off the tape recorder. Then he glanced at his watch. "By the way," he said and nodded at my hand, "what happened to your hand?"

Keep it simple, I thought. "Cut it on a broken glass."

He pressed his lips into a fine line, waiting for more.

I gave it to him, free of charge. "I knocked my car keys off the kitchen counter, and they fell in the trash. I forgot there was a broken glass in there."

He nodded. "That's all for now, Mr. Heidorn." He picked up the machine and groaned heavily as he stood up. "I'm sorry we have to do this at a time like this... Anyway, we appreciate your cooperation."

"Can I go now?"

The detective went over and opened the door for me. "Sure, you're free to go. You want one of the officers to give you a lift somewhere?"

I didn't know what to say to that. I didn't have anywhere to go. My mother's apartment, I guess. Pick up my things. And then what?

Crawl up inside that bottle and die.

"That would be fine," I said.

He gave me a solemn look and said, "I just want to say again how deeply sorry I am for your loss."

I wanted to tell him what he could do with his condolences, but I kept my mouth shut. I wanted that ride home.

ELEVEN

THE SUN WAS ALMOST UP when I walked out of there. A rookie patrolman drove me to my mother's apartment and on the way he told me all about how his girlfriend had recently kicked him out of their apartment. She'd caught him screwing one of her girlfriends, and now he was staying with his mother, too. I don't know how he knew I was staying with my mother—it was certainly none of his goddamn business—but I guess the police had nothing better to do than gossip. Anyway, he dropped me outside ma's apartment complex, and we wished each other luck. Then I went up the stairs and quietly let myself in.

Ma was still asleep. Still in her bedroom, anyway. I sat down on the sofa, feeling all wrung out and dead inside. I had no idea what I was going to do. Never in a million years could I tell my mother that her grandson was dead, that he'd died while I was out getting shitfaced in a bar.

Then the phone rang. And rang. Ma, wearing her ratty winter housecoat, shuffled out of her room, muttering groggily under her breath. She cut her bleary gray eyes at me and studied me like she wasn't sure who I was or what I was doing in her living room. Then she went into the kitchenette and answered the phone. She lit a cigarette at the same time.

Maybe I wouldn't have to tell her after all. Maybe that's

what this phone call was about.

I could hear the voice on the other end of the line. It sounded like my sister's voice. I guess I shouldn't have been surprised. Her husband was a retired cop. Word gets around.

I took a long breath and watched the blood drain from Ma's face. She turned and stared at me, her fist pressed to her lips, then she sank slowly into one of the kitchen chairs and made a long, horrible moaning sound that I will never forget.

My heart dropped into my stomach like a thirty-pound rock. I got to my feet, but my brains slopped around inside my skull, and I had to sit back down. I steadied myself and I got up slowly and walked over to the windows and pushed back the curtains. I wiped the fog off the window and stared out at the snow-covered parking lot.

No! No! No! No! she screamed over and over.

A long time passed. Ma didn't say anything. I rested my forehead on the cold window glass. I wished I was dead, too. Or if not dead, then at least passed out drunk in an alley somewhere.

"When were you going to tell me?" Ma was talking to me.

"I was gonna tell you…"

"I have to hear this from your sister?"

I stood there staring out the window and wondering what was coming next and how much worse the next thing would be.

"My God, out getting drunk while your son—"

"Ma…"

She kept her eyes away from mine and held out the phone to me. "Your sister…"

I walked across the room and took the phone.

"Anna."

"Al, my God. How could this happen?"

"I… We're not really sure."

"What was that poor child doing alone in that house? Why wasn't he with you… Or his mother?"

"I don't know, Anna. He was supposed to be with Sandy."

"I don't understand…"

"I don't either."

There was a long pause, then Anna said, "That poor child."

It went on like that for a while—"That poor child. How could this have happened?" Finally, I couldn't take it anymore.

"I got to go, Anna." I gave the phone back to Ma.

Ma didn't say anything for a long time, just stood there staring inwardly into some terrifying abyss. Then she slowly hung up the phone. For a moment, I paced the floor and wished I had some way to put us both out of our misery. I truly believe if I had had a gun on me, then I would have done it. We would all have been better off.

A long moment passed. Ma dried her eyes with a handkerchief and blew her nose. "Why wasn't he with his mother?"

She was like a goddamn broken record.

"What was that child doing sleeping in an empty house? What kind of mother allows that?"

"I don't know."

"You don't know!"

I looked toward the door.

A look of panic crept into her eyes. "Where's my granddaughter? Where's Donna?"

"She's fine, Ma. She's with Sandy."

"How do you know? When did you talk to her last?"

I tried to remember. "Yesterday."

She hugged herself tightly, like she was trying to keep herself from falling apart. "Why wasn't that boy with his parents?"

"I told you…"

"That poor child," she said, then she turned and glared at me, her eyes like burning coals. "That's why that officer was here last night. That's why he wouldn't talk to me—my own grandson!"

I got up and went into the bathroom. I closed the door and turned on the tap to mask the sounds of retching. My stomach heaved a few times, and I vomited into the toilet. Some of it got in the toilet, anyway. I took a drink from the tap and went back into the living room, trying to remember what I was doing there, why I'd come here.

Ma wouldn't look at me. That was okay by me. The phone rang again. I don't think she even heard it till the fifth or sixth ring. Word was apparently getting around town.

"Who is this?" she said. "Who?" She held the phone away from her mouth. "Somebody wants to talk to you. Somebody named Greg."

What the hell? I thought. "I'll take it."

Ma set the phone down so she wouldn't have to hand it to me.

I picked up the phone. "Yeah Greg?"

"Al, I just heard about your son. My god, I am *so* sorry."

"You heard..."

"Al, are you alright? Is there anything I can do?"

My mother had shuffled over to the sofa where she sat looking like an ancient mummy somebody mistakenly dug up.

"Do you want to talk?" he said. "I could meet you somewhere if you'd like."

"Now?"

"A thing like this—Christ, Al, I can't imagine. It might help to talk."

Talk? It might help to drink. It might help to get drunk and stay drunk. It might help to pick up a Louisville Slugger and beat the hell out of Russ and his fucking T-Bird. That might be of some benefit.

"Look Greg, I appreciate the offer," I said. "I really do. Now's just not a good time."

There was a slight pause. "Sure. I understand. I just don't want you to—"

"I know. Trust me, I know. Maybe tomorrow. We'll talk tomorrow."

"Sure." I could hear the disappointment in his voice. Here I was denying the poor bastard a chance to help someone, to get outside of himself, or however he would put it.

Greg said, "Well, if you change your mind, you know how to get in touch."

"I know." I hung up the phone.

Ma wouldn't even look at me. "That poor child," she cried. "He didn't deserve this family."

I crossed the room and grabbed my suitcase from behind the couch.

"Where are you going?" she said.

"Goodbye, Ma," I said, walking out the door. "Thanks for everything."

I had no intention of ever seeing her again.

Twelve

I DROVE BACK to the motel and sat in the station wagon in the parking lot, feeling sorry for myself, trying not to think about things because thinking about things was more than I could handle at the moment. One thing was certain, I would need a place to crash, to sleep off the big drunk I was planning on going on and staying on.

I went into the office and clapped the bell and waited for the motel lady to shuffle out on her canes. She didn't seem particularly surprised to see me. "Back already?"

"Looks like I'll be needing a room for the week after all."

She sighed heavily and lowered her bulk onto the stool, which groaned and creaked under her weight, but somehow didn't give out. It must have been a quality, American-made stool.

She flipped open the registration book and peered inside. "Is this what you do for fun? Check in and out of motels?"

I let that go without comment.

She pushed the registry at me. "Sign here."

I scribbled down my name.

"You can have the same room," she said.

"Perfect, the suicide room," I muttered under my breath.

She closed the register. "You know the rules. Fifty for the week."

"I don't suppose you'll give me any credit for—"

She gave me a slightly hostile stare.

"Never mind."

I took out my wallet, counted off four twenties and two fives. The whole time I could feel her cold, tiny, sunken eyes on me.

She started to lay the key on the counter, then hesitated. "You ain't planning on doing anything funny, are you?"

I leaned across the counter at her. "Are we talking about Jack Heidorn again?"

"I wasn't gonna say anything, but the way you been acting—"

"How have I been acting?"

"Like the other two who checked out in my motel this year. Wouldn't surprise me if there was a sign somewhere. Depressed? All hope lost? Kill yourself at Shaw's Motel! Affordable rates!" She fixed me with her mean little eyes and said, "You got that look about you. Just like they did."

I shook my head and set the stack of bills on the counter. "You got a hell of a sales pitch, lady." I picked up the key and went out the door.

I moved the station wagon in front of unit twelve. Home sweet home. Then I lugged my footlocker and suitcase back inside. I sat on the bed and felt my entire body shiver with exhaustion. The motel lady's comments had really unsettled me. I studied the walls and ceiling and carpet for blood spatter or stains. I didn't see any. At length my gaze rested on the footlocker, which held, among other things, my old Russian pistol. Maybe it was fate that I'd chosen this motel? I mean, what was stopping me? Did I think things were going to get better? Things were not going to get better. Best-case scenario, the cops would be too stupid to pin the arson on me, and Barker would somehow manage to keep his stupid mouth shut, and I would remain a free man, free to drink myself to death in some shitty motel room in a half-assed attempt to numb the pain. That shouldn't take too long. I already had one foot in the grave.

As I studied the footlocker, I could feel an icy wind blowing up my spine. The goddamn place was giving me the creeps. I picked up the keys and went out to the station wagon. It wasn't even noon yet.

I drove to a bar.

THE PARKING LOT at Chuck's was half full. I recognized four of the vehicles as belonging to regulars and there was Jack the barman's pickup truck, but I couldn't place the two Harleys. From time to time you'd have a gang of bikers try to turn Chuck's into a biker bar, but in the end Chuck's always turned out to be too depressing for them or the songs on the jukebox were too country or the clientele was too old and there were never any women around, and they would quickly move on.

It was a little after twelve-thirty when I strode into Chuck's. The jukebox was quiet, and the sound was off on the television. Four old timers slouched half dead at the bar. Circling the pool table were a couple of long-haired, bearded bikers I'd never seen before. They wore worn leather jackets with the name "Wind Tramps" embroidered on the back, and bandanas wrapped around their heads. It was a cooler uniform than the Steak N Shake guys wear, but it was still a uniform.

The regulars looked surprised as hell to see me. I guessed they'd heard the news by now. I took my regular seat at the bar, and Jack the barman came over and stood in front of me. He took the nub of cigar out of his mouth and nodded and pressed his lips together. "Goddamnit, Al, I don't know what to say."

"You don't have to say anything; how about bringing me a bourbon on the rocks?"

"Sure, Al. Sure."

I took out my wallet.

"Put that away," he said. "Your money's no good here. Not today."

One by one, the old timers looked over and muttered their condolences. Some of them even bought me drinks. Jack refilled my glass and said some guy had been calling, looking for me. He called several times, but wouldn't leave his name or number.

Johnny Law. Well, that didn't take long.

No, that was silly. The cops wouldn't be calling a bar. They'd be kicking down the door to my motel room, guns blazing.

Who then?

Greg?

No, he had no idea about Chuck's.

Barker.

Shit fire. I'd forgotten all about Barker. I still owed him a... thousand bucks. A thousand bucks for killing my son.

Well, let him try and collect.

I was on my third whiskey when I noticed a light snow had begun to fall. The whiskey was doing its job well, and I was feeling, if not at peace, then at least at home. Home. This was where I belonged. These people got me. What had six months of exile and sobriety gotten me? I was divorced, homeless, jobless, and I'd lost my only son.

The two bikers wandered over and introduced themselves. Butch and Rock, they said. The last thing I needed was chit chat. I pushed my glass across the bar for a refill.

"I got that," one of them said.

They said they'd heard on the news that the fire marshal suspected arson and they were curious if the cops had any suspects. Jack the barman shot them a dark look that had "Butt out" written all over it, but they were too drunk or stupid to pay it any mind.

I turned away and told them I'd come in here to forget about all that, not to hold a press conference. They nodded and backed off. Then I felt bad for biting their heads off like that, especially after they'd bought me a drink. I turned back and told them I didn't know about the cops, but I sure as hell suspected someone. This local colored boy.

"Yeah, which one?" Rock said. "What's his name?"

"Name's Eddie Grady. Why? You know him?"

The two bikers exchanged a look. "Not yet, we don't. You *sure* it was him?"

"I'm sure about one thing. I told the little bastard to stay away from my daughter and he swore he'd get even with me."

"That little bastard."

"Threatened to burn down my house."

"He said that?"

"Kids got balls," Butch said. "So, the cops arrest him yet?"

I shook my head. "Nah. If these cops had any brains, they wouldn't be cops." I slammed about half my drink. "The little prick just might get away with it."

The bikers exchanged another look. "Eddie Grady, huh?"

"Uh-huh."

They went back to the pool table, and I didn't think any more about it. I don't know why I told them that. I know why I told the detective, but I don't know why I told those biker punks that story. I don't know why I thought it was a good idea to blame that kid for something I did, except that I didn't like him being around my daughter and he was a convenient scapegoat.

Anyway, the last time I'd asked Donna about Eddie Grady she'd said that he'd moved away again. Back with his momma somewhere in Missouri. He apparently only stayed in Belleville when his momma was in county jail, then he stayed here with his grandma. It was a lousy thing to pin on a kid, but I figured he'd be fine at home with his momma... wherever the hell that was.

Thirteen

AROUND EIGHT O'CLOCK, the phone behind the bar rang. Jack the barman picked up and glanced at me and silently mouthed: "You here?"

I got to my feet and went around the bar. Jack held the phone to his chest, said, "It's him again," and handed me the phone.

Barker's toneless voice came on the line. "You stood me up, man. That ain't cool. Left me waiting in the park with my dick in my hand."

"I'm sorry. I forgot. My mind's been on other things."

"That's what I'm calling about. Them other things. We need to talk."

Everyone in the bar seemed to stare at me. "Not here, not on the phone," I said.

"How about we meet where we were supposed to meet, like four fucking hours ago?"

"Fine."

"Cool," he said. "The park then, in half an hour. And this time you best show the fuck up."

I started to say something, but he had already hung up.

I handed the phone back to Jack.

"Everything all right?" Jack said.

"Huh? Oh, yeah, everything's cool. Better get my tab."

"You ain't got a tab."

"That's right," I said. "Thanks."

"Take it easy, Al."

I should have known Barker wouldn't quit hounding me till he got paid. It didn't matter if he killed my son or not.

I was in no shape to drive, but it didn't stop me. You don't hire a taxi to take you to a secluded park to pay off an arsonist. Not if you got half a brain.

I parked on the south end of the pond, away from the ball fields, where there were still a few hardwood trees, pin oaks, maples, sycamores. An old beat-up bench had been dragged up to the road for some reason. The lone streetlight didn't work—probably busted out long ago by drug dealers or homos. I got out, sat on the hood of the station wagon, and smoked a cigarette as the wind blew the snowflakes around. In the distance glowed the soft colored lights on the houses and shrubs in the nearby subdivisions. If I hadn't been there to pay off a psychotic arsonist, it would have been a real nice, peaceful holiday scene.

I finished the smoke and angrily flicked away the butt. The more I thought about it, the more pissed off I got. The balls this guy had, coming around demanding money after he killed my son. Maybe it wasn't *entirely* his fault, but still... The guy had some fucking nerve. If I killed somebody's teenage son—even by accident—I'd feel like hell. I sure as shit wouldn't be hounding the grieving parents for money.

I thought about telling Barker to go fuck himself. Of course, if I did do that, he'd probably blow my goddamn head off. That's the thing with psychopaths—you never know what they'll do—though blow your head off is probably a pretty good guess.

I went around to the back of the station wagon and opened the tailgate, then I opened the footlocker and took out the cigar box. Inside was the Soviet pistol and a roll of bills. I pocketed a grand, then picked up the pistol and chambered a round.

I stared at the pistol for a long moment, then I put it back and closed the footlocker and slammed the tailgate.

There was still no sign of Barker.

I got to thinking what those girls had said about Barker, about him torturing helpless animals, about him beating some old guy half to death with a crowbar. I was all set to go back and dig out the Tokarev when a yellow Dodge Dart came tearing up the road, fishtailing on the icy roads, the one working headlight searching for pavement. Moments later, the Dart pulled up next to my station wagon, something unnatural blasting from the car stereo. There were two of them in the car, Barker and someone I couldn't make out. That pissed me off. I should have known a maniac like Barker wouldn't be able to keep his crimes to himself, that he'd want to share his depravity with the world.

One more person to testify against me. One more potential blackmailer.

I sat on the hood, hunched against the cold. Barker turned off the radio and eased out. The Dart's overhead light blinked on. In the passenger seat sat a girl, about twenty. It looked like it had been a rough twenty years.

"Stay in the car," Barker told her. He shoved his hands in his brown leather jacket pockets and strode up to me. "Hey man. How goes it? Making a dollar?"

The girl climbed clumsily out of the Dart. She leaned on the open door and scratched at her head. She had long, tangled hair and eyes with big black raccoon circles around them, like life had been using her face for a speed bag. She was bone thin like a lot of junkies you see who never eat anything but pills.

I nodded toward the girl. "What's this?"

"That's right. You two ain't met." Barker reached around and lovingly smacked the girl on her bony ass. "Say hi to Al, Bonnie."

Bonnie didn't look like she had the energy to speak. Her eyes looked as dead as billion-year-old rocks.

"Um, why's she here?"

Barker smiled. "I don't trust her out of my sight. That a problem?"

"Not at all. Just tell me how many people you're gonna let in on this. Have you sent out the press release yet?"

Barker laughed. "No need to worry about Bonnie. She's like six time zones away, man." He laughed again.

I wished I was six time zones away. I pulled the roll of bills from my pocket.

"What's this?" Barker said.

"It's what I owe you."

"Woah! Hold on there, Buckaroo. We need to talk."

My gaze shifted uneasily from Barker to the girl. I watched as her chin slowly dropped to her chest, then her head snapped back up. She glanced around with a mystified look on her face.

"I got your grand," I said. "What's there to talk about?"

Barker drew a pack of smokes and a chrome lighter from his jacket pocket. Bonnie stared drowsily at the cigarette in Barker's mouth.

"Gimme smoke," she slurred.

Barker ignored her. He took a long drag on his cigarette and said, "I'll tell you what's to talk about. You told me there wasn't anyone in your house. You said the place was empty. You remember that, don't you, Al?"

I stared absently out over the frozen pond. "That's what I thought—"

"Yeah, well I ain't so sure about that. You see, I been doing some thinking. I'm starting to think you knew there was somebody in that house. Someone you wanted to get rid of."

"Are you insane?" I cried. My voice startled me, the intensity of it. Bonnie stirred and glanced up at me, then her eyes clicked out of focus again. "You know that was my son in that house, right? Why would I want to kill my own son?"

Bonnie chimed in, her voice thick and slow, like a tape recorder with low batteries. "Sick fuck," she said.

"Shut the hell up," Barker told her. His eyes locked on mine, smoke curling around his lips. "I don't know why you done it, and I don't care. What I care about is you setting me up."

I swallowed hard. "Seriously? You really think that? You think this was all some kind of scheme to kill my little boy?"

Barker didn't say anything, but his eyes narrowed on me like blades.

"I don't even know what to say to that," I said. "I mean, that's just crazy." I held out the roll of bills to him. "Here's the other grand, like we agreed. Take it or leave it."

Barker smirked. "Now you're fucking with me, right?"

I sighed heavily. I could have kicked myself for leaving my pistol in the footlocker, for meeting this psycho alone in a dark, deserted park. Standing there, I felt stupid and exposed. But mostly stupid.

"Look, Mike, that's what we agreed to, remember? Two grand?"

Bonnie snorted.

"That was then," Barker said. "I'm looking at a murder rap now. I could be looking at life. The fucking chair, even. Imagine what that would do to Bonnie here if I got the chair? Poor thing, she'd be devastated."

"Devastated," she slurred.

I didn't know how to respond to that. Anything I said was just going to piss him off more. I didn't want to piss him off more. I wanted him to take what he was owed and leave me the hell alone.

I shoved the roll of bills back into my coat pocket. "So, what then?"

"Arson is two grand. Homicide is five."

"Five grand?"

"That's some echo out here," Barker said. "You're getting a bargain, man. Weekend before Christmas sale."

Barker hadn't shown any weapons yet, but I had no doubt he was carrying. Probably a whole arsenal. As for me, I wasn't so much scared as I was pissed off.

"So, you kill my 14-year-old son, and I'm supposed to pay you an extra three grand? Have I got that right?"

Barker shoved his hands into the back pockets of his Levis, the cigarette bobbing up and down on his lips. He took a few steps toward me and jabbed his index finger hard into my chest. "Don't you fucking try to spin this. That kid is on your head, not mine!"

I took a step back. My gut instinct was to punch him in his goddamn mouth, but I fought it for now. I guess I was still hoping I could reason with him.

"I'm gonna say it one more time," Barker said. "Homicide is five K."

He stared at me, like he was expecting me to pull five grand out of my ass. I tried to reason with him one last time, even though I was wasting my time. "Look, Mike, even if I agreed with you, where am I supposed to get another three K? It took me six months to save up the two grand."

"Not my fucking problem."

We'd reached an impasse. I didn't know what else to do but call his bluff. I reached into my pocket and went for the roll of bills again. "What do you say we quit dicking around? We had a deal. Now here's the grand I owe you. Take it or leave—"

I don't know what he hit me with. It could have been anything. A blackjack. The butt of a pistol. A sledgehammer. All I know is a galaxy of stars exploded in my eyes and I'm lying face down in the road, my nose pressed in the frozen gravel and my head feeling like a kicked-in Jack O' lantern.

"Fucking piece of shit thinks I'm fucking around," I heard Barker say. His boot connected with my rib cage and I groaned and closed up like a cheap deck chair. "Tell him I don't fuck around, babe."

"Mikey don' fuck around."

"I told you not to call me that."

I may have blacked out for a moment. When I came to, Bonnie was squatting beside me, clumsily prying open my eyelids with her sharp fingernails. "I think you killed him, Mikey."

"Yeah? Maybe. Who the fuck cares?"

"But... but, how're we gonna get the three grand if he's dead?"

I slowly blinked my eyes open. In Barker's hand was my Soviet pistol. He drew on his cigarette and studied the clip in his other hand.

"He ain't dead. His eyes just opened." He jammed the magazine into the grip.

I didn't think I would get up for a long time. When my vision finally settled, I was gazing at a pair of boots. Steel-toed. They weren't cheap boots either, so they were probably stolen. Barker put the toe under my ribs and flipped me over onto my back like a dead tortoise.

"Can you hear me, man?"

"Ungh," I moaned.

"Good. Here's how this is gonna go. You got till midnight tomorrow to come up with three grand. I don't care how you do it. Hold up a gas station. Borrow from a loan shark. Sell a kidney. What the fuck you need two kidneys for, ya greedy bastard?"

Bonnie snorted.

Barker pried the crumpled roll of bills from my grasp. "Midnight tomorrow. Oh, and don't get any ideas about running out on me because I *will* find your sorry ass if I have to stake out every bar on the continent."

He dropped my pistol next to my head. "Here, you're gonna need this to hold up that liquor store."

Then he hauled off and kicked me in the nuts.

FOURTEEN

I LEFT A MESSAGE FOR GREG TO MEET me at his cafe the next morning. I got there early and found a table in the back out of the way, where I wouldn't scare the customers. I must have been some sight with my black eye and busted nose. I spent a few minutes making a list on a napkin of all my possessions, anything I might be able to pawn or sell. The list turned out to be depressingly short. I still had my '72 Ford station wagon. That ought to be worth five hundred bucks—if I found the right sucker. There was my Tokarev TT-33, but the way things were going, I thought I'd better hang on to that. My LPs (Johnny Cash, George and Tammy, Barry Sadler, Merle Haggard, Tom T. Hall) were gone, burned up in the fire—not that they would've brought more than a few bucks and change. The bank had closed my checking account due to inactivity, and I had no savings to speak of. What little wealth I'd had was in my home, which was now, literally, ashes.

I crumbled up the napkin and limped over to the wastebasket. A grim, old couple stared at me like they'd never seen the walking dead before. I gave them a hideous smile and limped back to my table.

Greg had said he would be happy to meet me. I suppose he was afraid I'd fall off the wagon after what had happened.

He sure was in for a surprise.

I only wanted to see Greg because I thought it would give me a chance to hit him up for Barker's three grand. I'd have to come up with a good story, but all he could do was shake his head and give me that disappointed look I'd come to expect from him. On the other hand, he might write me a check. Stranger things have happened. Bob Ripley will tell you.

Only as I sat there smelling the coffee and the pastries, and my head began to clear, I wondered if I wasn't getting too worked up over Barker. Shit, what more could he do to me? I suppose, if you want to get technical, he could get some guys, track me down, break my kneecaps, cut off some fingers with a pair of wire cutters. Or simply put a bullet in the back of my head. He was on the hook for one murder. What was one more killing to a psycho like Barker?

That was the problem with violent crime. You weren't always dealing with the most classy and thoughtful individuals.

Anyway, I'd somehow managed to drag my broke ass out of bed. I figured I might as well make it worth the effort.

I got tired of folks staring at me like some kind of circus freak, so I went outside and had a cigarette. As I finished my smoke, Greg pulled up in his sleek '69 silver Jaguar, the kind of car that must make you feel like Sean Connery every time you slide behind the wheel. He parked on the far side of the street and stepped out of the roadster wearing a tan leather jacket and a pair of Ray-Bans looking like two million bucks. I, on the other hand, looked like I was in debt a couple thousand.

Greg removed his shades and crossed over. He pulled up and grasped both my arms and held me at arm's length. "Al, Jesus, how're you doing? Man, I am so sorry." He studied my face. "Christ, what happened to you?"

I shrugged. "It ain't as bad as it looks."

His face clouded over. "Ah hell. You've been drinking again, haven't you? Ah, Jesus."

"Sorry," I said. I wasn't sure what I was apologizing for.

And I didn't see any point telling him the beating had nothing to do with drinking. On the contrary, it was for something I'd planned while I was still on the wagon.

"No, no. Don't be. What you've been through—Christ, I can't imagine." He pursed his lips and nodded his head slightly. "I just wanted to see how you're doing."

"I'm okay."

"Sure you are. Jesus, I can't even begin—"

"I know. Thanks."

He pressed his lips into a fine line, and said, "If there's anything I can do—"

Here was my opening. "Actually—"

"Anything at all. You want to go inside, get some coffee... or tea?"

"No, not really."

We stood in a patch of sunlight on the sidewalk in front of the cafe for an awkward moment. A massive, gray cloud passed in front of the sun, and the temperature felt like it dropped ten degrees. It was probably a good idea to work up to it, make some small talk first before you hit a guy up for three grand. I asked Greg if he wouldn't mind walking over to the Pennys—assuming it was still open. With everything that happened, I had forgotten to buy my daughter a Christmas present. I wasn't really sure there would be a Christmas this year, but in case there was, I didn't want to screw that up, too. Greg was fine with that, so we started walking in the direction of the department store.

"How old did you say your daughter was?" he said. "Thirteen?"

"Thirteenish."

His face was grave. "How's she holding up? Have you spoken to her?"

I shook my head. "Not since..."

Greg nodded. "You're gonna talk to her, aren't you? Al, she needs to hear from you."

"Yeah. I'll talk to her. I don't know what I can say to her, but I'll talk to her."

"That's good. A time like this, a girl needs her father."

"Yeah."

Greg slipped on his Ray-Bans, and we walked for a while in silence. Tinny Christmas tunes oozed from outdoor speakers from the few remaining open shops. *Silver Bells. Little Drummer Boy.* All the tired, old chestnuts. Across the street I caught a glimpse of the Elvis impersonator busily working the gray-haired couple from the cafe. Served them right.

The Pennys, with its going-out-of-business sign, loomed ahead.

I said, "I asked her what wanted for Christmas? She tells me cash. Tells me she has an emancipation fund."

"Emancipation fund?"

"It's a long story. Anyway, I'm thinking maybe some perfume or earrings. A little purse, maybe. I don't know, whatever I get her she's gonna hate. I just think it's important I get her something."

Greg turned and gave me a troubled look. "Al, I know you've been through hell, but I was thinking… There's a meeting tonight. I'd be happy to come by, pick you up."

"I don't think so. Not tonight."

"Sure, I understand. But if you change your mind…"

"I'll let you know."

We crossed the street in front of the Pennys, and I followed Greg through the revolving doors and into the lobby.

I figured we'd made enough small talk.

"I got to tell you, Greg, right now booze is the least of my problems." I let that hang out there a moment as our eyes blinked around the store. Most of the stock was gone, along with the customers, all transported to the fancy new mall twenty miles north of town. We strode over to the perfume counter and cooled our heels while we waited for someone to acknowledge our presence. From the looks of it the clerks had gone out of the mall too.

Greg perched his Ray-Bans atop his head. "No, I get it," he said. "I can see how the program might not seem important now. Probably feels like your whole world's coming to an end. But times like these, that's when we can really use the support. Hell, Al, I'm not telling you anything you don't already know."

"Uh-huh."

"You gotta stay strong—and I'm gonna help you. We'll just take it one day at a time. One hour at a time. One minute at a time. I'm here for you buddy, twenty-four—"

"Can I help you?" Behind the perfume counter stood a young, dark-skinned dish with a high-wattage smile. She beamed at Greg for all she was worth. Me... I don't think she even saw me, not even with my horror show face.

"I was thinking about some perfume for my daughter," I said. "Nothing too fancy. She's only thirteen."

The clerk somehow managed to pry her eyes off Greg and turned to look at me. She did a pretty good job concealing her disgust. She nodded and drifted down the counter and came back with a small crystal bottle that she set in front of me. Teen Sparkle.

"This one is very popular," she said. "Would you like a sample? I could give you a little spritz on your wrist."

"That's all right."

"I'd like a spritz," Greg said.

She smiled coyly and gave Greg a spritz. He lifted his wrist and gave a seductive sniff.

"What do you think?"

"Nice. Kind of fruity. Reminds of that cereal... Fruit Loops."

I turned to Greg. "She likes Fruit Loops... to eat. I don't know about sprayed all over her."

"It's very popular," the clerk repeated. It must have been her whole sales pitch.

I gave a shrug and said, "Fine. Bag it."

I pulled out my wallet as the clerk wrapped up the perfume and placed it in a small green gift bag with red crepe paper. I paid cash, more than I'd wanted to pay, and Greg said goodbye to the clerk and we headed for the doors. Outside, we stood on the sidewalk and zipped up our jackets. Greg slipped on one of those flat woolen caps that rich Brits wear when driving their Aston Martins or whatever. Most people would look ridiculous wearing such a hat, but Greg somehow managed to pull it off.

"Any other errands?" he said.

I was just about to come out with it and ask for the three grand, when Greg cut me off again. "I really wish you'd come with me tonight."

"I'd like to, Greg, but... Well, the fact of the matter is, I'm in a bit of a tough spot right now."

Greg gave me a long, penetrating look. After a moment, he said, "Is there something you want to tell me, Al?"

"Well, the fact is, I've run into some—I guess you'd call it—unexpected expenses."

Greg kept his eyes on me for another moment, but said nothing. I turned and gazed off down Main Street at all the empty storefronts, courtesy of Greg.

"Is that why you called me last night?"

I shrugged.

Greg went silent. Silent and, I thought, a little distant.

After a long moment, he cleared his throat and said, "We should be getting back."

We started back in the direction of the cafe. I had to pick up my step to keep pace. Well, I'd managed to screw that up somehow. I was trying to think of some way to turn things around when Greg said, "Are you asking me for a loan, Al?"

"No," I said. "I mean, just a small one."

We walked on some more. Across the street, the Elvis impersonator called out to us. This time, we ignored him. Greg's brow was furrowed, and he looked deep in thought.

"When you say unexpected expenses," Greg said, "you mean for the funeral and things like that?"

Christ, I hadn't even thought about that. A casket. A plot. Mortuary bills. How much was all that going to set me back? We were probably talking hundreds, if not thousands, of dollars.

And who was making the plans, working out the details, meeting with the undertaker, mortician, or whatever you call him? There was probably a cemetery director, too. It wasn't three thousand bucks I needed. It was more like twice that.

Well, shit, one crisis at a time. And right now, Barker seemed like the bigger, more immediate crisis. He was crazier and a lot more dangerous, anyway.

"All that stuff adds up," I said.

There was a lull.

"Al, I don't think I've ever asked you... Do you even have a job?"

"Actually," I said with a shrug, "I'm working on that."

The sun had dipped below the tops of the empty buildings, plunging our side of the street in deep shadow. It was suddenly so cold it made my front teeth hurt.

"Tell you what," Greg said. "What's the name of the funeral home? I'll give them a call. Maybe I can do you some good."

I stopped in my tracks, but Greg didn't seem to notice. I had to hurry to catch up with him. "That's okay," I said. "I wouldn't want you to go to any trouble. Maybe, you know, if you could just see clear to loan me—"

"No trouble," he said. "I know most of these funeral directors in town. Which one is it?"

My shoulders slumped as I felt the air go out of me. Well, that was it. I figured I may as well stop the charade.

"The fact of the matter is... It's not for the funeral. I mean, there's that—but there's other things too."

"For chrissake, Al."

He sounded like he'd had it with me. I guess I couldn't really blame him. "What other things?" he said.

What other things? I thought. All I'd been able to come up with was some lame bullshit about an emergency operation. A liver transplant or something, but knowing Greg, he'd want to talk to my doctor first.

I shrugged. "I can't really go into it."

Greg's cafe came into view. On the street a meter maid was scrawling tickets. Something pale yellow bloomed beneath my wiper blade. I glanced over at Greg's Jaguar. No ticket.

Suddenly, Greg halted and turned to look at me. "Al, why don't you come to the meeting tonight?"

I crammed the little gift bag into my jacket pocket, crumpling and tearing the paper. "I mean, I'd like to tell you about it, but… I promised not to." I studied Greg's face. I could tell he had moved on.

I said, "So? What do you think?"

"About a loan? I don't think so."

"But—I thought you were here to support me."

"I am. In your sobriety. Not financially."

"I thought you had this thing about helping other people?"

"Sure, but I'm not convinced this would help you. It might even hurt you. I mean, it's hard to say for sure when you won't tell me what it's for."

I sighed and nodded in defeat. I felt like a real jackass for asking. I wouldn't have felt that way if he had said yes, but now… now I felt like a complete ass.

"You're right," I said. "You're right. I had no business asking."

Greg put his hand on my shoulder and fixed his eyes on me. "It's just that the last thing you need is someone bailing you out. I'd be doing you a disservice. You need to take hold of your life, Al. With both hands. Work things out for yourself. Am I right?"

"Um…"

"I have faith in you, Al. Whatever life throws at you… I know you can beat it. And I'll do everything I can to support you."

"Except financially."

His lips pressed tight in a rigid smile. "Correct."

He gave me a friendly pat on the arm and again offered his condolences and said I should call him any time, day or night, if I felt myself backsliding. Then he said, "You sure you won't change your mind about the meeting tonight?"

I shook my head. "Another time."

Greg pursed his lips and slowly nodded, then he turned and started across the empty street. He gave a small wave as he drove off.

I glanced up at the clock over the closed Bank of Belleville. If the clock was right, I had fourteen hours to come up with three thousand bucks.

FIFTEEN

ROB A GAS STATION, he says.

Sell a kidney, he says.

See a loan shark, he says.

What did I know about loan sharks? I might have seen something in a movie once, a gangster flick, years ago. Did they even exist in our town, in this day and age? Or did you have to go to some big city? And then what? Look in the yellow pages under loan sharks?

I was definitely out of my league here.

I thought, you know who would know about loan sharks? Barker. I should have asked him while he was splintering my ribs with his steel-toed boots.

Normally when I have problems, I can't resolve on my own I head over to Chuck's. You can have your Ann Landers and Dear Abby if you want real, constructive working-class advice you got to talk to the bartender in a dive bar.

I got to Chuck's around lunchtime. Lucky for me I wasn't hungry. If you asked Jack the barman if they served food, he'd always say, "Nah, we only serve drunks." Besides, internal injuries and thoughts of imminent death have a way of suppressing your appetite.

I nodded to Jack as I hobbled in and took a seat at the bar.

He drifted over and studied my face.

"Jesus, Al, what happened?"

"Minor accident," I said. "I'm fine though. Really."

Jack shook his head. "Shit man, you've had a rough couple of days."

"You got that right," I said. "How about a bourbon on the rocks?"

This time nobody offered any condolences or offered to buy me drinks. In fact, they pretty much treated me like a pariah. Maybe they thought I was cursed or something. That was okay by me. I nursed my bourbon and bided my time till the lunch crowd thinned out. Then I called Jack over.

"Got an unusual question for you."

"I doubt it."

"You wouldn't happen to know any loan sharks?"

Jack considered for a moment. "Something to do with the accident?"

"What accident?"

"You... Forget it."

"A friend of mine needs a couple grand."

"Uh-huh." Jack looked thoughtful. "I could make a call. Might do you—I mean your friend—some good."

"I'd appreciate it."

Jack nodded. He leaned in close. "These people, they ain't exactly your community credit union types, know what I mean?"

"No, I figured that."

He studied me for a moment, then he shrugged and shuffled over to the phone and made the call. It was a quick one. He came back and pushed a scrap of paper across the bar. "Here's the name of a shylock—"

"That's his name? Sherlock?"

"Shylock. It means loan shark. Jesus Al, are you sure—"

"I'm sure. A hundred percent."

Jack frowned. "He says you can come over now."

"Like right now?"

SO MANY THINGS TO BURY

"That's what he said."

"Okay then," I said, getting to my feet. "Where am I going?"

"You're gonna meet him at The Bounce House."

"Bounce House? You mean... the strip joint?"

"Yeah. That's his club," he said. "I told you this ain't no credit union."

I studied the scrap of paper. The guy's name was Mike Ochello. The name meant nothing to me, but then I didn't spend a lot of time in the local underworld. I thanked Jack, who said don't thank me, then I went out and got in the station wagon and headed toward the river.

I'd driven past The Bounce House hundreds of times. It sat just off Route 3 on a dusty stretch of industrial, a gaudy neon funhouse set down among a row of blighted 1930's warehouses. I'd never been inside; strip clubs were for frat boys, bachelor parties and pathetic, lonely old men. I was working up to being a pathetic, lonely old man who went to strip clubs, but I wasn't quite there yet.

It was a twenty-five-minute drive. A pink and blue neon sign buzzed and blinked over the parking lot, which was empty except for a few mounds of piled snow. The club's sign featured the pink outline of a nude woman, bent over, brandishing her neon backside. I pulled onto the lot and sat there with the motor idling and the radio turned down low to a country station, staring at the former warehouse, turned "gentleman's club," and telling myself there had to be some other way. But if there was, I sure as hell couldn't think of it. There was no time to sell a kidney, and as for robbing a gas station—just because I'd hired an arsonist to burn down my house and he'd killed my son, that didn't mean I was ready for a life of crime.

I eased out of the station wagon and walked across the parking lot. The front doors were unlocked. Inside, the club was dark and quiet and smelled of cigarette smoke and stale beer. I felt dirty and—I must say—a little aroused just being there. I glanced around the joint, at the mirrored walls and half dozen round stages, some booths, a few tables, a bar and a DJ station. I looked for strippers, but I didn't see any. There wasn't anybody around. It was Sunday; maybe they were all at church. It wouldn't surprise me to learn that strippers went to church.

A head popped up from behind the bar. "We don't open till four," a thirty-something man said. "How'd you get in here?"

"I'm here to see Mike Ochello."

He studied me from behind the bar—the black eye, the broken nose. "Yeah? What about?"

"Business."

"What kind of business?"

I frowned heavily. I had to really struggle to keep my cool. "He's expecting me."

He leaned his elbows on the bar and fixed his eyes on me. "And you are?"

"Name's Al."

"Al," the guy said, like he didn't believe a word of it. "Okay, Al. Have a seat in a booth. I'll tell Mike you're here." Then he paused and said, "And don't touch nothing."

I glanced around the club. What the hell wasn't I supposed to touch? The booze, I suppose. God, I must have really looked desperate for a drink.

I slid into one of the booths and tried to act like it was the most natural thing in the world for me to be visiting a loan shark at a strip club on a Sunday afternoon. I searched my pockets for a pack of cigarettes, but I didn't have any. Maybe I'd smoked them all. I thought about what happened to my cigarettes for a while, and then I wondered if they'd forgotten about me. Then my thoughts took their usual paranoid turn. I started imagining all kinds of things, like maybe they'd called up some hoodlum friends to come over and beat the crap out of me and take my money and they were just waiting for them to arrive.

Of course, that was crazy. If I had money, I wouldn't be seeing a loan shark.

Some more time passed and still nobody appeared. I was

about to get up and walk out when a rear door opened and out came a short, middle-aged man in a blue, two-toned police uniform.

What the hell was this? A set up? Maybe I had been right to be paranoid.

"Al?" he said.

I got up, ready to make a run for it.

The cop put out his hand. He was short, but he looked tough. Like little Jimmy Cagney tough. "Mike Ochello. Good to meet you."

I forgot about my hand till it was too late. Mike Ochello had a strong, wound-opening grip. I bit back a cry.

"You're a cop?" I said.

He laughed. "Chief of police, yeah. I also own this club. How's that for covering the bases?"

"Impressive, I guess."

He was studying my various cuts and bruises, but he didn't remark on them. Real class. Instead, he asked if I wanted a drink.

I always wanted a drink, but I wanted to get down to business even more.

"No, thanks."

Ochello slid into the seat across from me and reached behind him and grabbed an ashtray. He removed a pack of Lucky Strikes from his shirt pocket and fired one up and offered me the pack. I helped myself to a smoke. My hand hurt like hell. I could feel the blood flowing under the bandages.

"So, how long have you known Jack?" he said.

"Jack? Couple of years. Since he started bartending at Chuck's."

"Good people, Jack. He said you wanted to do a little business. So, what are we talking?"

"Three grand."

Ochello nodded and blew smoke toward the darkened ceiling tiles. "That's definitely doable. No problem. What're we talking for collateral?"

I hadn't thought about that. Collateral. "Well, there's…" I nodded toward the front doors. "I got this vehicle…"

"Yeah. I saw you pull up. Unless I'm mistaken, that old jalopy ain't worth more than a couple hundred bucks, and that's being generous."

He was being very generous, but I kept that to myself.

"Own your home?"

I shook my head. "No."

Mike Ochello nodded and leaned back, draping his arm along the top of the booth. "So… Al… What do you do?"

I folded my hands on the table in front of me. "I've done a lot of things. When I was in the army—"

"Yeah? Where'd you serve?"

"Korea."

"Same here. What regiment?"

"Seventh Cav."

"That was Custer's regiment, wasn't it?"

"Uh-huh." It was great we were bonding, but I tried to get back on topic. "I'm a pretty good mechanic. My expertise is foreign cars. Volkswagens, mostly."

"Seventh Fleet, myself." He looked thoughtful. "Wasn't the Seventh Cav involved in some crazy shit over there? Bunch of civilian gooks killed?"

I shrugged. In thirty years, nobody—I mean nobody—had ever mentioned No Gun Ri to me. And this wasn't the time nor the place to swap war stories.

"Happened all the time over there." I blew the smoke out and shrugged before I spoke again. "I worked in a stove factory right out of the service. I've laid carpet. Done some roofing. Exterminator."

"I could use a good exterminator." He glanced around the club. "This place is overrun with fucking cockroaches. Big as rats. Thank God, we ain't got no rats. They'd probably be as big as dogs."

I crushed out my cigarette.

"So what you doing these days?" he said.

"I'm kind of between jobs."

Ochello frowned. "Uh-huh. What else you got collateral-wise?"

I shook my head. I couldn't come up with a damn thing.

A phone rang somewhere. The bartender strode out of the back room, hefting a couple cases of Budweiser. He set the cases down on the counter and answered the phone.

"Hey Mike, it's your better half."

"Tell her I'll call her back."

"She says it's important."

"What'd I just say?"

Ochello tapped the ash from his cigarette into the tray. "Our loans are for three months, Al. We spot you three grand, you got three months to pay back plus the three points. The three points you pay every Friday."

"Three points?"

"Comes to ninety a week."

"Okay."

"We're talking a total of…" He paused to do the math. "Four eighty."

"And I got three months."

"You got three months for the three grand. The points you pay every Friday."

"Those are the terms?"

"Those are the terms. You had collateral, you might get better terms. What can I tell you?"

He might as well have said a million bucks in three months. It would take me two years to save up that kind of cash.

Ochello took a drag on his cigarette. "You a bettor, Al?"

"Not really."

"Most of my clients are players. A player can make three grand in three hours—if he's good. Course, if he was good, he wouldn't need me—you see what I'm saying?"

"I think so."

Ochello fixed his dark eyes on me. He seemed to be searching for something in my face. "You're the guy who lost his boy in that house fire a few days ago."

I stared back at him. I guess I wasn't really surprised that he'd heard about it. This guy seemed to know all my deepest, dark secrets. It was creeping me out.

"My condolences."

"Uh-huh."

Ochello regarded me for another moment, then he slowly shook his head. "I can't do it."

"What?"

"Can't do it," he said. "You seem like a decent guy, Al."

"You're the second person who's said that…"

"I've been doing this long enough to know you can't pay me back, and I don't want to send somebody to collect. That's no good for anybody, you know what I'm saying?"

I didn't say anything.

"You just lost a kid. You don't need no more grief."

I nodded. I could tell Ochello had already moved on.

He stood up and stuck out his hand. "Nice meeting you, Al. And I'm real sorry for your loss."

He offered his hand, and I put mine out there for him to mangle. Then I watched him cross the floor and disappear into the back room.

"Huh," the bartender said with a short laugh. "That's a first. Never seen Mike turn someone down for a loan before."

I sat there for a moment, half-stunned, trying to think of my next move. I was pretty sure my next move involved something with a lot of alcohol in it.

Finally, the bartender cleared his throat.

"Hey pal?" he said.

"Yeah?"

"*Why* are you still here?" he said.

Sixteen

ON THE WAY back to the motel, I stopped at a gas station and got a fifth of bourbon. What a relief to be done with the charade of sobriety. Well, I'd proved to myself that I could do it if I wanted to, if I had to. Only I didn't want to and didn't have to. Never again.

I poured myself a glass of bourbon and sat on the edge of the bed, trying to think. But I couldn't stop thinking about my boy and what his last few moments must have been like asleep in that coal bunker. I wondered if he'd heard the upstairs window shatter, the bottle of gasoline explode across the floor, the fire jumping around upstairs. I wondered if he'd awakened and tried to feel his way out through the broiling, smoky darkness, only he couldn't. Or if he'd slept right through it. I'd read somewhere that when a house burns the victims are almost always found dead in their beds. It's not the fire that gets them, it's the CO that poisons the blood.

The cop said they'd found Frank in the basement, so maybe he died in his sleep. Maybe he never knew what hit him.

I hoped to God it was like that.

I switched on the black and white television and watched an old holiday movie. *Miracle on 34th Street*. Around midnight, I drifted off, a good drunken dreamless sleep. I slept till 11 o'clock when I was awakened by someone pounding on my door. I sat up, bleary-eyed, my tongue thick and heavy in my mouth.

"Housekeeping!"

"Not now!" I said. "Come back later!"

"When?"

"Later!"

She mumbled something and went away. I glanced around the room for some hair of the dog, but found only dead soldiers. I got out of bed and shuffled into the bathroom and took a piss and a long drink from the tap then I crawled back under the sheets. On the end table, next to the alarm clock, sat a little green bag. Slowly, the cobwebs cleared from my brain, and I remembered things.

Donna's Christmas present.

Barker.

The three grand.

I threw off the blanket and crawled out of bed. I got dressed and pulled on my coat and stepped outside under slate gray skies. The air was so cold it felt like it was cutting into my lungs. I reached in my pocket and counted my coins—enough for one short phone call. I started walking down Main toward the phone booth.

I stepped inside the booth and dialed Russ' number. It rang three times before Sandy picked up.

"Lemme talk to my daughter."

"You got some nerve calling here!" Her voice was shrill, with a slight manic edge to it.

"Donna. I wanna talk to—"

"Murderer! That's what you are! A murderer!"

"What? What are you talking about?"

"You think I don't know what you did? Setting fire to our house? You think you're gonna get away with it?"

"I don't—"

"You think the police don't know? I told them what you did!

I hope they lock you up for the rest of your miserable, pathetic life!"

She'd rattled me for a second. How *could* she know? It wasn't possible. No way could she know. She had a hunch, maybe, but she had no proof. Her guilty conscience was probably eating at her, making her imagine all kinds of crazy shit that just so happened to be true.

I got my back up. "You're nuts, you know that? You're crazy as a… a…"

"You come anywhere near Donna, I'll call the *po*lice! If I don't shoot you myself!"

Okay, now she was starting to piss me off. She and her stinking fiancé were as much to blame as I was. Finally, I laid into her. I let her have it. "Listen, you bitch, you wanna know whose fault it was? Why wasn't Frank home with you that night? Who kicked him out of the house? Was it me? Was I the reason he was sleeping in that empty house? You listen to me, if anyone's to blame, it's you—you and that rotten son of a bitch cousin of mine!"

I heard Russ' voice. "Gimme that."

Russ came on the line. "Al, do us a favor. Don't call here anymore. And don't come to the wake today. You didn't help pay for it, so you don't need to come. Just stay the hell away, okay? I mean it."

The line went dead.

I slammed down the phone. Then I slammed it down again. And again.

Christ, I hadn't thought about the wake. But I'd be goddamned if I was going to let that cheating bastard tell me what to do. Besides, Donna would be there. It would give me a chance to talk to her.

I walked across the icy parking lot and went inside the gas station. The same clerk was working behind the register.

"Where's the booze?" I said.

He looked at me. "We don't carry any."

I glanced around the store. Sure enough. Nothing but soda pop, Gatorade, and Snapple. There wasn't much food-wise either, a few bags of chips, some beef jerky. Candy bars. I grabbed a couple of Baby Ruths, thinking the peanuts might have some nutritional value, and I went to stand in line. The old woman in front of me had two cartons of cigarettes and a handful of lottery tickets. The staples of modern life. While I waited for her to finish rooting through her purse for some cash, I looked the place over. How hard could it be to hold up a joint like this? Pull out my semi-automatic and shove the barrel under the clerk's chin. *See this? I snapped a gook's neck to get this, so you don't want to fuck with me. Now gimme whatcha got in the till.*

Poor kid would shit his pants. He wouldn't think twice about being a hero or dying for Gulf Oil. The three-thousand-dollar question was whether it would be worth it. I had a hard time believing they had much cash in that register. Not this place. A few hundred, tops. I'd have to hold up a dozen gas stations.

I paid for the candy and chewed one of the bars as I made my way back to Shaw's Motel. I was too strung out to sit in my room waiting for the wake to begin. I needed movement, so I got my things and went out to the station wagon. The engine was slow to crank, so I let it sit awhile. On the third try, it turned over. I drove the streets aimlessly, up and down Main. I had less than twelve hours to come up with three grand.

Who was I kidding? I wasn't going to come up with three thousand bucks in that amount of time. I wasn't going to come up with three *hundred* bucks.

Once I stopped fooling myself, I felt like a great weight had been lifted off my shoulders. A great sense of relief. Of calm, almost. Like a guy with terminal cancer after he's reached the acceptance stage.

Let Barker come after me. Let him try. I'll be ready for him. Seriously, what was worried about? I survived Korea, I could survive a psychotic little punk like Barker.

SO MANY THINGS TO BURY

Chuck Inn was dead, as you might expect at noon on a Monday—or pretty much any other time. I went in and took my regular stool. Jack was behind the bar, scratching something on a clipboard. He didn't ask me how I'd made out with the loan shark, and I didn't bring it up. He made me a drink and went back to taking inventory while I went to work on my bourbon, killing the hours till my son's wake.

Later, I drove back to the motel. I went through my stuff and got out my one and only suit—the same black double-breasted suit I'd worn to my wedding almost twenty years before. It still fit; if anything, it hung a little loose. It was decades out of style and smelled like mothballs and stale sweat, but it was a suit and that's all that mattered. I dug out my pair of black loafers and gave them a quick spit shine and put on a white shirt and the suit and a dark blue tie. I grabbed Donna's gift bag and then I drove to the funeral home.

I pulled into the parking lot, but I wasn't quite ready to go inside. Not yet. Across the street was a dive bar called The Top Hat. An old man's tavern. Probably the only bar in town I had never been in. It seemed like the ideal time to rectify that. I grabbed my things and crossed South Illinois Street and went inside the tavern. There were plenty of open seats at the bar.

Behind the bar stood the oldest bartender I had ever seen by a good twenty or thirty years. He had to be ninety if he was a day. The old man shuffled over and studied me with blue watery eyes, but didn't say anything, just rolled his false teeth around in his mouth like he was chewing a big chaw of tobacco. I ordered a bourbon on the rocks. I took a swallow and said, "Guess you get a lot of clientele from the funeral home."

He got his teeth adjusted the right way and said, "Can't say as we do."

"Guess it's just me then."

The old man stared at me a second—not in an unfriendly way, not in any way really—then he shuffled off.

Over by the door, a middle-aged woman with a pug face and

a poochy belly stood yelling into the payphone. She argued with someone named Trisha, probably one of her unfortunate children.

There was no one else in the bar.

The woman hung up the phone and came over and sat down next to me. "What a little cunt," she muttered. She lit a cigarette and asked me if I had any kids. I didn't want to start a conversation with her, but I couldn't see any way out of it, so I mumbled I didn't. She said I was lucky. I nodded and kept my eyes on the back bar and sipped my drink.

She said, "My name's Sal."

"Uh-huh."

"Short for Sally."

"Nice."

She nodded at the gift bag on the seat next to me. "Who's the present for?"

"Hmm? Oh, my daughter."

"I thought you said you didn't have any kids?"

"Oh. I lied."

"You lied?"

"Yeah. I lie all the time. I even lie about lying."

She studied me for a moment, then she threw her head back and roared with laughter. She laughed like she'd just drowned a puppy.

I slammed the rest of my drink, paid, and picked up my bag and got the hell out of there.

I found Donna in the corridor outside the room where they had my son in his casket. She wore a little black dress and looked like it was the end of the world.

"Hey sweetheart," I said. "How're you doing?" I gave her a hug. I could have been hugging a frozen fence post.

"Sandy doesn't want you here," she said cooly.

"Yeah well, it ain't her wake." That didn't quite come out the way I'd meant it to. I said, "What else did she say about me?"

"She told the mortuary guys not to let you in. They said as long as you don't make trouble, they gotta let you in."

"Damn right," I said.

She turned to go.

"Oh hey," I said, holding out the gift bag. "I got something for you. Merry Christmas."

She lifted her eyes and stared up at me. "You're giving me a Christmas present at my brother's funeral?"

"It's a wake, not a funeral. Besides, I might not see you on Christmas Day." I shoved the bag at her. "Go on, take it."

She pushed it away. "I don't want it!"

"It's perfume."

Her eyes snapped angrily. "I said I don't want it!"

"What am I supposed to do with it?"

"I don't give a shit!"

I let my hand fall to my side. "Fine," I said. I went over to a trash can and tossed away the present. Fifteen bucks down the crapper.

My daughter turned and started to walk away.

"Hang on a second."

Donna hesitated. For a while, neither one of us spoke. I didn't know what to say. Then all the sudden an idea came to me. A way I could make up for all the stupid and terrible things I'd done. A way I could make things right. We could start over—the two of us—someplace new. A fresh start. What did I have to lose? What did either of us have to lose?

"How'd you like to go away with me?"

"What?"

"I'm serious. Tonight. We'll swing by your place and grab your things."

"Go where?"

"I don't know. Someplace. Alaska. Florida. Wherever you want to go."

She stared at me. "You're drunk."

"Then you can drive."

She turned to walk away, and I went after her, grabbing her by the arm. She jerked away and screamed that I was hurting her.

I turned her loose. Suddenly, there were people in the hallway staring at us. Staring at me, anyway.

"Why not?" I said. "Weren't you just asking to move in with me? For chrissake, what's keeping you here?"

She pointed down the hall. "My brother's in there!"

"Okay, then after. We could go after."

Her eyes welled up and her little mouth started bubbling up and down.

Ah shit.

"It's the middle of the school year!" she said.

"They got schools everywhere."

"Why would I go anywhere with you? Why would anyone go with you?"

I lowered my voice slightly, hoping she'd follow my lead. "I thought you didn't like living with Russ? Isn't that what you told me?"

She glared at me. "Since when do you care so much about me?"

"I've always cared."

"You're so full of shit!"

This time, I dropped my voice to a whisper. "Can we not make a scene in the hallway?"

"Get away from her!"

I knew that voice. Sandy stormed down the corridor. At her side was my two-timing, rat bastard cousin.

"You leave that girl alone!" she cried. "Haven't you done enough?"

I wanted to punch her in her goddamn face, but I took a slug at Russ instead. The blow caught him off guard and he dropped like a sack of wet laundry.

"That's for Frank," I said.

Sandy let loose with a high-pitched scream, then she was on me, scratching, pounding my chest and my face, her nails raking my flesh. I got her off me and my head swiveled around for Russ; he was still down on the floor, rubbing his jaw.

Somebody took my arm. "Sir, we need you to leave—"

I shook the cold-hearted bastard's hand off me. "That's my boy lying in there!"

A second man, substantially larger, latched onto my other arm. "Let's go," he said gravely.

"I haven't got to see him!"

"And you're not going to."

They got me up under the armpits and lifted me off my feet and carried me toward the exit.

"Fine! I'm going! Get your dirty hands off me."

They carried me through the back doors like a rag doll. Talk about humiliating. Once outside, they released me. They stood there, arms folded, barring the door. I glanced around the mostly empty parking lot. Where the hell was everybody? The lot should have been filled. That was my boy in there.

I started down the steps and made my way to my vehicle. I'd be goddamned if I was paying for half that wake now.

As I got to my car, somebody called my name. I turned and scanned the parking lot. From the driver's window of a yellow Cutlass Supreme, an arm beckoned to me. The arm belonged to that detective. Hill.

"Al Heidorn. Got a second?"

I guess I should've known I hadn't seen the last of him. My jaw tightened as I walked over to the Cutlass.

The detective made a thorough study of my face. "Jeez, you've had a rough coupla days."

I stared at him. "Is this about what happened in there?"

"Why? What happened in there?"

"Nothing."

He nodded toward the mortuary guys. "Nothing? That why them fellas eighty-sixed you?"

There was a long pause. "Is there anything else?" I said.

He took a sip from a Styrofoam coffee cup. "Yeah. I thought you might want to know. The fire investigator finished his report. Your house... It was arson, all right."

I nodded. "Arrest anyone yet?"

"Soon. Very soon."

"You talked to my ex-wife."

He looked at me.

"She's got some crazy ideas," I said.

"Your alibi checked out, Al."

I felt my asshole tighten. "Well then, I won't keep you." I turned to go.

"Oh yeah, one more thing. That black boy you said threatened to burn down your house? Eddie Grady?"

"What about him? He confess?"

"Not to me," the detective said. "They found him out on Gilmore Lake Road. What was left of him. If he hadn't been a colored boy, we might never have identified him. Turned out all the others were accounted for."

I stiffened, just for a moment. That kid wasn't supposed to be here! He was supposed to be... somewhere else. Why would Donna tell me he'd moved away if she knew he...

Oh.

I pictured those two bikers at Chuck's, the ones who were so interested in who I thought torched my house. Christ, you couldn't say anything without people going off half-cocked. I guess they were going to blame me for this, too.

I glanced back toward the funeral home. The undertakers stood in front of the doors, staring back at me, then they nodded and went back inside.

I turned back to the detective. "What's that got to do with me?"

"I'm not a hundred percent sure."

"Then I don't want to keep you."

The detective pursed his lips. "Just thought you'd like to know." He drained the last of his coffee and said, "See you around, Al."

I waited till the detective had driven off, then I climbed into the station wagon. I sat behind the wheel and forced myself to breathe. Everything felt dead inside me. For a long time, I stared at the doors to the mortuary.

It should have been me in there.

SEVENTEEN

THERE WAS A NOTE waiting for me back at the motel. It had been slipped under the door. I turned on the lamp and sat down on the bed. It was written on fine linen stationery. The handwriting was fine, too.

Dear Al,
I tried phoning you this morning. Your mother said you were no longer staying with her, so I took a chance that you had gone back to the motel. The manager of the motel said that was indeed the case. The reason for this note is to say that I hope you are doing well, and I trust there are no hard feelings. I hope, too, that I can stay on as your sponsor. Please feel free to give me a call anytime. I am always available to talk on the phone or in person. That's one of the perks of being the boss.
All the best,
Greg

I crumpled up the note and tossed it in the wastebasket with the rest of the trash.
On the way back to the motel, I'd made up my mind. I was getting the hell out—with or without Donna. And the sooner the better. I thought about what Barker had said about coming

after me, tracking me down, whatever. If it was somebody like Ochello threatening me, I might be worried, but Barker was nothing but a two-bit hoodlum who would probably find his ass back in jail before the end of the month. Besides, what was the point hanging around here any longer? The whole reason for coming home was to try to win back Sandy and try to get back into my kid's good graces, and maybe get my house back.

I'd say mission accomplished.

I got out of my suit and into some old clothes, jeans and an old black hooded sweatshirt. I crammed a few dirty shirts and undershorts and a toothbrush into my suitcase and put the suit and loafers away in the footlocker. I picked up the near-empty Jim Beam bottle and sucked it dry, savoring the last few drops on my tongue, then I tossed it on the bed for housekeeping to deal with. It was the motel lady's lucky day. No suicides to clean up after.

This time, I didn't bother checking out. It was my room for the week, whether I was there or not.

I drove toward the highway. I had no particular destination in mind, just as far away from town as I could get. Maybe I'd just disappear. Why not? Not a soul in the world would miss me. Except maybe Barker and that detective. But they'd get over it.

West or east? North or south?

Not Texas, that was for damn sure. None of them Bible Belt dry counties either.

Alaska? Had I been serious about going there? Sure, it's cold as a polar bear's asshole, but at least...

I slammed the brakes. The station wagon fish tailed and skidded to a stop in front of the Catholic church.

Alaska. What was it Frank had said? Something about Russ having a couple thousand bucks in rare coins. Frank was going to get his hands on them, coins and run off to Alaska...

Was it two or three thousand? I couldn't remember, but it could have been.

I sat there in front of the church, smoking a cigarette and

drumming on the steering wheel, trying to decide my next move. The idea of robbing that two-timer certainly had its appeal.

Not living in fear of Barker had its appeal, too.

Goddamn it, I needed time to think.

I turned the station wagon around and drove back to the motel. Lucky for me, I hadn't checked out after all. I had some thinking to do.

I lay on the bed and smoked a half a pack of cigarettes. Slowly, a plan came together in my head. A simple plan for a simple man. They'd be at the wake till closing time, maybe longer—nine or ten o'clock—that should give me plenty of time to get in and out. Assuming there were no surprises.

And if there were surprises? I guess, like all things, it comes down to luck. You're either lucky or you're not. I can't say I've been particularly lucky in this life. Then again, I was certainly overdue for some good luck.

I put on my boots and went out to the station wagon.

Maybe I wouldn't have to skip town after all.

EIGHTEEN

THE FIRST THING I did was to stop at the dollar store and buy a wool ski mask and a pair of cloth work gloves. Then I drove to my cousin's house. It was the Sunday before Christmas and a fine mist hung over everything. Normal folks were home digesting their dinners in front of television sets tuned to football or *Frosty the Snowman*.

And then there were us not-so-normal ones.

I circled the block a few times in the station wagon. The sidewalks were empty, not even a solitary dog walker. I parked on an empty side street a block from Russ' house, leaving the engine running, then I slipped on the ski mask and gloves. It was 8:30 p.m.. I was cutting it damn close.

After the shitkicking I'd gotten from Barker, I wasn't taking any more chances. I got the pistol out of my footlocker and slipped it into my waistband. Nothing sobers you up quite like cold Russian steel on your groin. Then I walked down the iced-over alley, hoping none of the neighbors picked this time of night to take out the trash. I passed a half dozen working class bungalows, some dark, most with a few lights on. I pulled the ski mask down over my face. Had this been any other time of the year, my mask and gloves and dark clothes would have screamed rapist or burglar, but in late December I only looked a little suspicious.

Russ' home fronted 22nd Street, a busy collector road. You couldn't have asked for a lousier setup. The houses sat nearly on top of each other. In back of his house ran a narrow alley and across the alley sat the backyards of more bungalows which faced a private road. Russ' place was near the center of the block, so windows gazed out in all directions. It wasn't all bad. I caught a break with the weather, anyway. The sub-freezing temperatures had frosted and fogged most of the windows, and it was so cold there wouldn't be a lot of dogs out, dogs whose idiotic barking would draw attention to my presence.

It looked like I'd caught a break. The lights were off in Russ' neighbor's house, and the driveway was empty. I turned in at Russ' garage. I went around the side of the bungalow and looked for a basement window I could squeeze through. The windows were small, but not too small for a scrawny frame like mine. Old cheap window glass covered by a flimsy screen. No bars or thick glass blocks to deal with. The first screen I tried popped off easy as a bottle cap. I pushed on the window, but it must have been locked from the inside. I didn't know any quiet way to break a window, so I waited till a loud car passed by on 22nd Street, then I put my boot through it. You'd think I busted a plate-glass window at Penny's. Glass crashed like a pair of cymbals and rained down on the basement floor. Two or three neighborhood dogs started up.

I peered into the dark basement. I might have been staring into the Black Hole of Calcutta. I couldn't make out a thing. I picked some of the bigger, more scary-looking shards out of the window frame and tried to ease my way through. I lowered my feet through first, but I was getting the hell cut out of me on the broken glass. It didn't seem like it should be this hard, crawling through a window. But everything was hard. Even the simple things. How would a real professional do it? It was probably a trade secret. Finally, I said to hell with it, took a deep breath and launched myself feet-first through the window. I landed on some kind of folding table. The table collapsed beneath me, and I crashed heavily and noisily to the cement floor.

My pistol skidded across the floor.

For a moment, I lay flat on my back on the collapsed table, waiting for the breakers of pain to subside in my back and my arms and legs. I must have got the attention of every dog in a two-mile radius.

I slowly got to my feet. My ribs, my elbow, my hand, my knee—everything hurt. I couldn't see two inches in front of my face. A burglar with any brains would have brought a flashlight, or at least a small penlight. I could've got one at the dollar store for less than a buck. I fished around in my pants and found my lighter. That gave me about as much light as a firefly's ass. For the next few minutes, I stumbled around in the darkness looking for the pistol, knocking into shelving and bicycles and tripping over cardboard boxes and cracking my shin on old desks and dressers. I couldn't very well leave a Soviet semi-automatic pistol behind; might as well leave a signed confession. I felt along the rafters till I found an overhead light bulb and pulled a chain and the basement lit up. I mean, what the hell. After all the noise I'd made, what was a little light? I found the pistol under a shelving unit, covered in cobwebs. I shoved the gun into my waistband and limped toward the staircase. That's it, I thought. One more mishap, one more piece of bad luck, and I'd throw in the towel and get the hell out of there.

Halfway up the stairs, it occurred to me that the basement door might be locked. I turned the knob, and, to my great relief, the door opened. I found the light switch and crossed into the living room. The upstairs definitely had that septic tank smell; I couldn't see how Sandy could stand it. The next thing I noticed was the huge Christmas tree, a fake fir, in a corner of the living room by the TV. Under the tree were a few gifts wrapped in dull red and green paper. I wondered if some of them were for Frank. I recognized a number of the ornaments on the tree. They were mine from when I was a kid. There was one in particular that I had made in grade school, a little penguin crafted from a pine cone and a ping-pong ball and...

Headlights washed over the living room windows; I froze on my feet till the lights moved on.

Goddammit, focus!

Frank had said the coins were in Russ' desk. I had no problem finding the desk; it was an antique roll top number, the kind with all them cubby holes. The bottom drawers were locked, and I hadn't thought to bring a crowbar. I could have won an award for world's worst prepared burglar. I went back to the basement and poked around, looking for something to jimmy open the drawers. I found an old wooden tool bench with lots of tools dating from the Great Depression, all covered in a thick layer of Roosevelt-era grime. I found everything but a crowbar. I settled on a dusty hammer and chisel and ran back upstairs.

It was closing in on nine o'clock. They'd be pulling up any time now. My hands were shaking, but I went to work on the bottom drawers, breaking up the wood around the locks. The work was maddeningly slow. That desk must have been solid oak.

I hacked at the drawers a long time before I got one open. Slowly, one by one, the wood gave way, and the drawers opened—but there was no sign of a rare coin collection. Fact is, I didn't find a single thing of value—just stacks of ledgers, old letters, ancient photographs, a couple pairs of broken reading glasses and some tobacco tins containing miscellaneous keys, bullets and pins. I searched the other rooms for a second desk, but there wasn't one. Maybe Russ had grown suspicious and hid his treasure from the kids.

I stood in the middle of the living room holding a hammer and chisel and hating myself for being such a stupid, hopeless bastard, when a truck with a bad muffler pulled into the driveway. My throat tightened. Well shit. Do I make a run for it out the front door... or do I stay... force Russ at gunpoint to hand over the coins? Maybe he's got a couple grand squirreled away somewhere?

The problem with that was Donna would be with them, and I didn't want to mess her up her any more than she'd already been. Sandy was right. I'd done enough damage to my children.

Then again, if I didn't get those coins, the consequences could be far worse than a little trauma. For me, anyway.

I tossed the hammer and chisel behind the Christmas tree and turned off the lamp and got down behind the sofa. I slipped the Tokarev from my waistband and waited.

It seemed to take forever for them to get from the truck to the back door. At length, the door creaked open, and I heard them clomp up the kitchen stairs, talking. Sandy seemed agitated about something. She called out Donna's name.

There was a pause, then she called out Donna's name again. That was odd. I figured she would be with them.

Maybe she hadn't come in yet.

She called Donna's name again.

"She isn't here," Russ said. "She probably left with one of her friends."

"What friends? Anyway, she would've told me."

"Okay. What do I know?"

They moved around some more, taking off coats, hanging things up, then Sandy said she was going to check upstairs. The steps groaned under her weight. The refrigerator door opened and a beer can popped, then heavy footfalls came toward the living room. The TV blinked on not five feet from me. An old black and white movie, something Christmasy with Bing Crosby. As I crouched there, a painful cramp began working its way up my left leg. Getting up was going to be a bear.

Russ, meanwhile, got comfortable in a recliner and hawked up something and swallowed it so it wouldn't go to waste. A moment later, Sandy came back downstairs. There was a note of concern in her voice.

"She's not here. She hasn't been home."

"How do you know?"

"I know."

"What?"

"I know!"

"Did you check the machine? Maybe she left a note in the kitchen."

I glanced at the answering machine. The light wasn't flashing.

"I looked. There's no messages."

On the television, Crosby and Danny Kaye were doing a feather dance and lip syncing a song about sisters or something.

"How can you sit there watching television?" Sandy cried.

"You're getting yourself all worked up. If you ask me, she probably went home with Al."

"Al left at four o'clock."

"He could have come back, couldn't he?"

"She wouldn't have gone with him."

"Why not?"

"She just wouldn't!"

"Well, I don't know what to tell you."

There was a pause. "What if something happened to her?" Sandy said.

Her words hit me like a jolt of electricity. I felt my pulse thump out from my chest into my arms and head.

"What could happen?" Russ said.

I thought about that. Would Barker do something that stupid, that reckless?

Hell yes, he would.

"I don't know how you can just sit there when my daughter is missing," Sandy cried.

The old man got up and turned off the television. "Who says she's missing?"

"If anything happened to her—"

"Oh, for Chrissake, if you're so worried, let's call the police."

I didn't want to go through with it. I wanted to drive out to Barker's place—or wherever he was hiding out. And if my daughter was there...

I'd get the coins just in case. I'd gone this far.

I saw the dish of that sticky, hard Christmas candy on the end table. I grabbed a handful of that and stuffed it under my mask and into my mouth to disguise my voice.

Sandy said, "I'm going to go look for her."

"Look where?" Russ said. "Where are you gonna look?"

I stood up then, slowly, painfully, my thigh cramping up something awful. Sandy's face crumpled with fear, and she let go a small cry. I think I gave them both the fright of their lives. I was surprised Russ' ticker didn't give out. Instead, he got to his feet and went over and stood beside Sandy while she clutched at his arm. Her hero.

I leveled the pistol at Russ' big gut. "Nobody moof," I said.

He stepped in front of Sandy and gave me a hard scowl. "What the hell is this? How'd you get in here?"

I gagged and couldn't talk. I guess I'd overdone it with the candy.

"You're making a big mistake, fella."

I stepped out into the middle of the room and motioned with the barrel of the pistol toward the sofa. "Yoo," I said to Russ, "'i 'own."

"What'd he say?" Russ said. "What? I don't understand. What language is that?"

"Where's my little girl?" Sandy cried.

That threw me for a moment. Suddenly I wasn't just an inept burglar with a mouth full of rock candy, I was a kidnapper too. Or worse. Whatever I was supposed to be, this wasn't the time to get into it.

"'own, ea ya," I said.

Russ scowled. "What have you done with the girl?"

I reached under my mask and spit the candy into my hand, then I tossed it away. "I ain't tellin' ya again," I said. "Sit!"

Neither one of them moved. They were proving to be as stubborn as a pair of old mules. Finally, I said, "There's nobody here, okay? The house was empty. Now sit down!"

Sandy slowly perched on the edge of the sofa, while Russ

stared at the Tokarev. "That's a Russian pistol," he said.

My God, how the hell did he know that? Who the hell knows a Russian gun when he sees one? Sandy knew I had a Russian pistol. I wasn't sure what Russ knew, but Sandy sure as hell knew.

"Never mind," I said. "Where d'ya keep the valuables?"

Russ looked at me blankly. "Valuables? What are you talking about… Valuables?"

"What've you done with my daughter?" Sandy cried.

I stared at the two of them. "Quit stalling. The coins. Let's have 'em."

That's when he noticed the desk. Russ turned back to me, his eyes like two smoldering coals. "What'd you do to my desk, you son of a bitch? That was my father's desk!"

I think he was more angry about his stupid desk than I was about Sandy selling my entire house. I raised the barrel, chest high. "Last chance…the coins."

"Look pal, I don't know where you got this idea about coins. Somebody must have given you some bum information. The only coins I got are the ones in my pocket, and you ain't getting those either."

This was bad. I hadn't counted on the bastard being so pigheaded. I mean, I knew Russ was a foul-tempered tightwad and a bully, but most bullies are cowards. That's what they say. I figured given the choice between dying a hero and some stupid coins, it would be a no-brainer.

Unless he was telling the truth about the coins.

I hadn't considered that—that Frank had made the whole thing up. Now that I thought about it, the boy always did have a complicated relationship with the truth.

No. That wasn't possible. Who'd make up a story about rare coins? Russ had to be bluffing. He had the coins all right, and I was going to get them—or I didn't know what.

"I ain't telling you again," I said. "Let's have them coins."

I moved toward them, finger on the trigger. The old man

didn't even blink. He wasn't rattled in the least by me or my Soviet death machine.

"You get out of here now," he snarled. Then he turned and crossed the room toward a small end table with a drawer. I had a pretty good idea what was in that drawer—and it wasn't coins.

Things were happening too fast, I was losing control of the situation. Not that I'd ever had much control.

"Don't move!" I yelled.

He went for the drawer. The son of a bitch was begging me to shoot him.

"Don't do it!"

His hand went in and came out with a large caliber handgun. He left me no choice, and I pumped two shots into him. Both hit him square in the chest. The room filled up with smoke and powder. Then Russ let go of the handgun, staggered sideways a few steps and toppled backwards into the Christmas tree. The tree crashed down on top of him. Sandy stood frozen, mouth open in a silent scream.

I could see it in her face. My gun. My voice. My size and height. My torn black hooded sweatshirt. The way I knew about the coins.

Sandy slowly raised her arm and crooked a finger at me. She started to say something, but she never got the chance. I must have been operating on auto-pilot because I don't remember pulling the trigger, though I must have. I remember the first shot hit her in the guts. I don't know about the other one. I may have missed.

Sandy lay in a fetal position on the floor, moaning, whimpering, O god, O god, over and over.

I gazed at her as she writhed, moaning on the floor. I almost felt sorry for her. I wanted to say something, something that might explain my actions; I owed her that much. But I couldn't come up with any words. And, besides, there wasn't time.

I ran out the back door, past the garage with Russ' T-bird tucked safely inside, and on down the alley. Lights were going on all over the block. I slipped on a patch of ice and went down hard, but I got to my feet and hurried on. At the street, I slowed to a steady, inconspicuous walk till I got to the station wagon. I slid in behind the wheel and thanked God I had had the sense to leave the engine running. I swallowed a big gulp of air, and then, with everything I had left, pounded my head repeatedly on the steering wheel.

"Goddamnit! What the hell is wrong with people!"

I waited till the stars dimmed in my eyes, then I got the hell out of there.

Nineteen

I DROVE ACROSS town to one of the low-rent neighborhoods and turned down a string of back alleys till I found a row of dented trash cans. I dumped the ski mask and gloves, then I drove back to the motel.

Why hadn't I stayed in Texas? Why the hell had I come home? The boy had begged to come stay with me. We could have rented a duplex somewhere on a little dead-end street. I could have taught him to drive. Not through the front door of the house, but normal driving. Why had I come back? *Why? Why? Why?*

I pulled around to the back of the motel where the station wagon would be out of sight, then I stashed the pistol in the glove box. The smart thing would have been to toss the gun off a bridge somewhere, get rid of the evidence, only I still had Barker to deal with. And I wasn't about to meet up with him unarmed. Not again.

I changed into a pair of jeans and my work jacket and walked down the street to the phone booth. I dialed Barker's number. Once again he took his sweet time answering.

"If you took my daughter I will fucking kill you," I said.

There was a lot of noise in the background. A loud stereo or hi-fi was playing. Like somebody was throwing a party.

Barker laughed. "You mean Donna? Don't worry, man. She's in good hands. Bonnie's looking after her. They're getting to be real tight."

His words hung in the air. I had a death grip on the phone.

"If you touch one hair on her head..."

"You got only yourself to blame, man. We didn't want to pick her up, but you weren't taking this seriously." He paused. "Have we got your attention now?"

"I want to talk to her."

"People in hell want a sodie pop," he said. "Look man, nothing's gonna happen to your little princess as long as I get paid—tonight."

A moment ticked by.

"So what about it? You got the three grand?"

"I got it," I said through clenched teeth.

"Excuse me?"

"I got it!"

"That's what I like to hear." He paused. "You know she came willingly. Bonnie was like, you want to get high? And she was like, fuck yeah..."

Somebody, an obese twenty-something guy wearing a hooded coat, rapped on the glass of the phone booth. Surprised the hell out of me. I caught my breath and turned my back to him. He knocked again, harder. I pushed open the door and shouted, "Do you fucking mind? I'm on the phone here!"

He had the blank expression of a big, dumb ox, and that somehow made me angrier still.

"You almost finished?" he said.

"I'll be finished when I'm finished." I slammed the door.

From outside the box I heard his muffled voice. "Every time I try to use the phone you're in there..."

Barker said, "Who the fuck you talking to?"

"Nobody. I'm in a phone booth. Where do you wanna meet?"

"Which one?"

"What?"

"Which phone booth?"

"What the hell's it matter which phone booth? What are you looking for me?"

"I don't have to look for you. I got something you want, remember?"

Yeah. He didn't have to look for me.

I took a long breath. "Where do we meet?"

"At the park. Same spot. Eleven sharp. And come alone."

He hung up.

The dumb ox rapped on the glass again. I flung open the door and rammed my shoulder into his big gut. He stumbled backward and called me a string of four-letter words. I kept walking back to the motel.

I stood across the street in the shadow of a sycamore tree and made sure no cops were staking out my room. Then I went into my room and lay on the bed and chewed my thumbnail, seething, trying not to think about what Donna must be going through.

An emergency vehicle went by on the street, siren shrieking. I almost leapt out of my skin. Any moment now I was expecting the police to surround the motel, some guy with a bullhorn telling me to come out with my hands up. Even our hick cops were bound to connect the arson to the double homicide. It was all a matter of time.

But right now I didn't want to think about any of that. I only wanted to figure out how I could get my daughter back, in one piece. Nothing else mattered.

I glanced at my watch. Quarter to ten.

The more I thought about it, the more I knew there could be only one way out of this.

Greg's Jaguar.

I left the motel and hoofed it back to the phone booth. I spent more time in that goddamn booth than I did in my room. I was out of change, so I had to buy a pack of cigarettes at the gas station. With the change I dialed Greg's number but he didn't pick up, so I left a message on his machine. The gist was that I was going through a real hard time, that I was backsliding pretty bad. I may even have faked a few sobs, a catch in my voice, although I didn't have to fake much because, truth be told, I was a goddamn mess. I let him know where he could find me.

I didn't even want to think about what would happen if he didn't show.

Ten o'clock. One hour till I was supposed to meet Barker. I hurried back to the station wagon and searched under the seats till I found a roll of duct tape. I made sure the semi-automatic was cleaned and loaded.

Then I drove to the park.

TWENTY

AFTER I LEFT THE PARK, I drove straight to Chuck Inn. Jack was leaning on the end of the bar, laughing it up with a craggy-faced woman who had a laugh that sounded like a head-on collision. Over at the pool table were the same two bikers, who, if I had to bet, had something to do with the killing of Eddie Grady. With all the bodies piling up, I'd forgotten all about Eddie Grady.

Jack drifted over. "Hey Al," he said. "The usual?"

I nodded, and Jack went to make my bourbon on the rocks.

I stared at the hockey game for a while and nursed my drink. Of course, everything depended on Greg now, on him getting my message and being the conscientious A.A. sponsor I thought he was. And if it turned out he wasn't, if he'd decided he'd had enough of my crap... So be it. I was prepared for that too.

I tuned everything else out—the jukebox, the hockey game, the clink of billiard balls, the dull murmur of the regulars—and I went over in my mind how things would go. I tried to account for everything that could possibly go wrong. But of course, you can't. You can account for maybe twenty-five percent, tops. If there is one thing you learn from heist movies, it's that the number of things that can go wrong is infinite.

And every once in a while, you get lucky.

I glanced at the clock over the bar. I still had fifty minutes to kill. The phone behind the bar rang. Jack answered it on the first ring, cupped his hand over the mouthpiece, and looked at me and whispered, "You in?"

I nodded and got up and went around to the end of the bar.

Jack handed me the phone. "Says his name's Greg."

I took the phone. "Yeah Greg."

"Al, I got your message. I wanted to make sure you were still there."

"I'm still here."

"How're you doing, pal? You okay?"

"Oh, you know…"

There was a brief silence. "Al, what do you say we meet at that little cafe next to the fairgrounds? You know the one I'm talking about? Grumpy Joe's?"

I wondered if he owned that diner, too. "I don't know, Greg. I don't think I ought to be driving."

"Sure, sure. Then how about if I swing by and pick you up?"

"I guess that would be all right."

"Fine. I'll be there in a half hour."

"Can you make it any sooner than that?"

"Um, I can try," he said. "Just take it easy, okay Al?"

I gave the phone to Jack and went back to my stool and ordered a refill.

"Take it easy, he says."

"What's that?" Jack said.

"Nothing." I lit a cigarette and walked down to where the two bikers were playing eight ball and slamming pitchers of draft beer and acting like nothing happened, like their hands weren't dripping with an innocent kid's blood. I strode down to the far end of the table. "Fellas," I said. "Got a minute?"

"What's up, man?" the one called Rock said.

"Got a question for you."

The other biker chalked the tip of his cue. "We didn't have nothing to do with it." I thought he might have given me a wink, but I wasn't sure. Then he lined up a shot and called the six ball in the side pocket and missed.

"It ain't about that," I said. "What d'you say we step out back? Just take a second."

The bikers exchanged a suspicious glance.

"You'd be doing me a favor," I said. "It'll only take a minute."

They looked at each other again, then the one called Rock turned to me. "You ain't no fucking perv, are you? I mean, I hope to God you ain't no fucking perv."

I shook my head and faked a laugh, then I mouthed the word, "Dope."

"Who the fuck you calling a dope?" he said.

"No... I wasn't... I mean, I want to *buy* some," I said.

Jesus, this guy *was* a dope.

Butch looked to his friend and shrugged, and said, "I'll go." He tossed his cue on the table and grabbed his leather jacket and we went out the back door. Just outside the door sat two bikes, a Harley and a Triumph. Except for the bikes and Jack's pickup and my station wagon, the lot was empty.

"Did you really say dope?" Butch said.

"Yeah, I'd like to buy some. I thought you might know someone."

He gave me a curious, half amused look. "Seriously, you ever done drugs before, old man?"

"All the time."

"Uh-huh. Like what?"

"You name it," I said, trying to remember the names of the drugs my fellow alcoholics used to name-check during A.A. meetings.

"Fuck man, you can't even name a single—"

"Pot."

"Pot," he repeated.

"Cocaine. Speed."

He grinned and shook his head. "Okay, grandpa, you want to score some weed, is that it?"

Tires crunched on gravel. A police cruiser pulled slowly down the alley and the biker stared at me, startled, like I had planned something with the cops. The patrolman behind the wheel glanced at us briefly, but he didn't slow.

"Friend of yours?" Butch said.

I shook my head, and we waited nervously till the cruiser rounded the corner.

Then I said, "Not weed. I was thinking more like, you know, cocaine."

Butch breathed into his cupped hands to warm them. "So, you're a cokehead now? If I didn't know any better, I'd say you were a narc."

"I'm not a narc."

"Cause if you are a narc, you gotta tell me. It's entrapment if you don't."

"I'm not a narc." I wasn't sure what a narc was, but entrapment is something cops do, so he must have thought I was a cop. He looked dumb enough to think that. "Look, I don't need a lot," I said. "Just, I don't know, about thirty bucks worth."

He broke into a snaggle-toothed grin. "What's the matter, old timer? Jim Beam ain't doing it for you no more?"

"Something like that."

"You're a trip," he said, and studied me for a moment. "You're serious?"

"Uh-huh. What do you say? Can you help me out or not?"

"Shit, you think I walk around with bags of coke in case some old barfly wants to get jacked up?"

"Look, if you don't have it, just say so."

We lapsed into silence. I was about to head back inside when the biker scanned the parking lot and said, "Wait here."

He strode over to the Harley. It was a damn fine machine. A low rider 1200, classic black and chrome. He probably had to sell a lot of dope to afford the payments on that thing. He popped open a small compartment under the seat and withdrew a sandwich bag and a snub-nosed revolver. He slipped the revolver into the back of his jeans and stuffed the bag into his jacket. Then he walked back to where I stood and pulled a corner of the plastic bag from his pocket, the bag containing some kind of white powder. "This will cost you fifty."

"I only need thirty—"

The baggie went back into his pocket. "We ain't negotiating here. Take it or leave it."

I opened my wallet and peeled off two twenties and a couple of fives. I'd be lucky if I had enough left to pay my tab. I held out the bills to him.

Butch scowled. "Jesus, man, can you be a little more conspicuous?"

He snatched the bills from my hand and tossed me the sandwich bag. I almost dropped it.

"Don't overdo it," he said. "That shit will make your heart explode." He turned and walked back into Chuck's.

After he was gone, I leaned up against the station wagon, weighing the baggie in my hand. You sure didn't get much for fifty bucks. I opened the bag and took a little sniff. It had a slightly flowery scent to it, or so I imagined. I figured I'd see what all the fuss was about and took a pinch between my finger and thumb, like it was snuff, and snorted some up my nostril. It burned going up and down, like sniffing Drano, only it didn't taste like Drano. It tasted more like Play-Doh.

I leaned against the wagon, wondering what the big deal was...

And then it hit me.

It was hard to describe the feeling. It was like, I don't know, like I'd just got some really, really good news. Which, of course, I hadn't. But you could have fooled me.

I could see what he meant by my heart exploding, though.

I smoked a cigarette to calm myself, then I went back inside the bar to wait for Greg.

Twenty-One

GREG SHOWED UP at 10:30 on the dot. Reliable as an old Swiss watch, he was. I still didn't know what to do about him. Everything was all jumbled up in my mind. I was just so goddamn relieved and grateful that he showed up. I figured I'd deal with that if and when the time came. Right now, the only thing that mattered was getting my daughter back. After that, I didn't much care what happened.

Greg stopped and exchanged some small talk with one of the regulars—probably old friends from his drinking days—then he took the stool beside me. Jack the Barman came over, but Greg waved him off, then he turned to me and launched into his prepared statement, telling me how it would have taken superhuman willpower to keep sober after what I'd been through and how he was glad I called, that a lot of guys in my situation wouldn't have. It showed I was making real progress. I had to choke back a cold, bitter laugh; the guy *really* was clueless. Greg glanced around the bar, taking in the pathetic cast of regulars and the loud bikers working the pool table. He looked as comfortable as a guy getting a prostate exam. As for me, I was still feeling the coke and the booze and feeling pretty good considering what lay ahead of me. I offered Greg a smoke. He shook his head then polished off my drink, keeping one eye on the clock while Greg talked himself hoarse. He kept trying to drag me to some diner with him. I stubbed out my cigarette and sat there, not saying a word.

After a moment of silence, Greg said, "You're not still sore about that loan?"

"Hell, I've forgotten all about that." I called Jack over and I paid my tab, then I stood up and grabbed my pack of smokes.

It was time.

"Look Greg, I appreciate you coming out. It means a lot to me, but something just came up, something I got to attend to right away."

Greg gave me a puzzled, slightly annoyed look. "I don't get it. You don't want my help? Then why'd you call me? Why'd you have me come out here?"

"Like I said, this just came up a few minutes ago."

"What came up? What comes up at ten o'clock on a Sunday night?"

I shrugged. "This thing, well, it's kind of important."

He waited a minute. "Does this have something to do with…"

"What?"

"With whatever it was you couldn't tell me about the other day?"

I shrugged. "You might say that."

Greg stared at me with a puzzled frown. "You're not driving?"

I nodded toward the front door. "I sure as hell ain't walking in this."

"Let me call you a cab."

"Cab won't work."

"What d'you mean it won't work? Why won't it work?"

"Trust me, it won't work."

He sighed and dropped his eyes to my face. "Then let me drive you."

I looked at him for a moment and rested my hand on his shoulder. "Too dangerous. Besides, you've done enough already." I paused and said, "Don't think I don't appreciate it."

"What's too dangerous?"

"Forget it, okay?" I gave his arm a pat and turned, then I turned and staggered toward the back door.

"Hang on," Greg said, getting to his feet. He caught up with me at the door. He took hold of my arm and leaned in confidentially. "Al, I can't let you drive in your condition."

"You're not my Greg, father. I mean, you're not my father, Greg."

"Lemme give you a ride."

I stood against the wall studying the ancient floorboards, which drifted in and out of focus, pretending to weigh his offer. "Fine," I said at length. "Just remember, this was *your* idea."

"Come on," he said.

I followed Greg out to the back lot. I could hardly believe it worked, that he seemed to go along with it.

Then again, we were just getting started.

The temperature felt like it had dropped twenty degrees since I'd stopped by the park that evening, and that didn't even take into account the warming effects of all the bourbon I'd drunk. The air felt like it wanted to snow again, and here and there, a few stray flakes floated on a light breeze. Greg's '69 Jaguar gleamed under the vapor lights, waiting for us, waiting for something to happen.

Greg said, "We'll take my car."

"If you say so."

He unlocked the car doors, and I eased into the passenger seat. Christ, that was some ride. Those leather seats felt like you were sitting on a million bucks. Not crisp new bills, but soft, old money. Greg started the engine, which purred like a snow leopard or some other exotic, nearly extinct species of cat, and we pulled out onto Main Street.

"You're gonna have to tell me where to go," he said.

"Citizens Park."

He stared at me, his mouth pinched in a puzzled frown. I knew what that look meant; it meant only queers or drug dealers went to Citizens Park at 11 o'clock on a Sunday night.

"Hold on, Al. I... I don't want to be involved in anything illegal."

"Don't worry, you won't be," I said and paused. "Besides, this was your idea to drive, not mine."

I waited for Greg to pull over and order me out of his vehicle, but that didn't happen. He kept driving. God knows what was going through his mind. After a long moment, he said, "Al, I need you to tell me what's going on here."

The park was still a good three miles away. I knew Greg was only going to put up with so much dancing around. "It's not what you think," I said. "We're going to pick up my daughter."

"Your daughter? Your thirteen-year-old daughter? In a park...at 11 o'clock?"

"You got to trust me."

"Yeah, you keep saying that."

An orange city truck approached, tossing salt on the road. Greg suddenly pulled over. This is it, I thought. He's kicking me to the curb. Then the truck rumbled by and he pulled back onto the road and we drove on again. He was just trying to keep his roadster from getting splattered with salt.

Some time passed before he spoke again.

"I want to trust you, Al, but what's that little girl doing in the park at 11 o'clock on a December night?"

"Waiting for me."

Greg sighed heavily. "Let's cut the bullshit. I need you to tell me what's really going on."

I'd strung him along as far as he'd go. It was time to come clean. "What's going on is I owe some scumbag three thousand dollars."

It got real quiet in the car. There was an extended silence, then Greg said, "That's why you called me tonight. This was never about funeral expenses, was it?"

"If I don't come up with three grand, there could be a lot more funeral expenses."

Greg's face clouded over. "Al, goddamnit, enough with the riddles!"

"I'll pay you back—every penny. You want interest? I'll gladly pay interest. Whatever you want. It might take me some time, but you know I'm good for it."

He waved his hand dismissively. "Fine. You don't want to tell me, don't. It doesn't matter." There was a slight pause. "Al, I can't give you three thousand dollars. I can't give you *three* dollars. We've been all through this."

"Okay. Fine. You want the truth? I'll give you the truth."

And I did. I gave him the whole story—all except the parts about shooting Russ and Sandy, and the part about that black kid and the bikers. Those parts I left out. They were what you might call incidental to the story. But I told him about my ex-wife selling the house and about Barker and the fire and about Frank getting kicked out of Russ' house and about how everything went terribly, horribly wrong. I told him about my daughter's kidnapping and, finally, the ransom, or whatever you want to call it.

Greg took it all in silently. Meanwhile, we kept driving slowly, ploddingly toward the park. The wipers brushed a thin coat of snow to the side of the windshield.

"Jesus Christ, Al. Jesus Fucking Christ."

"I know. This isn't exactly what you signed on for, is it?"

Greg's eyes wavered. "You know you're looking at a murder rap. Murder. Arson. You know that, right?"

I stared ahead. If he only knew.

"That poor kid," he said. "What she must be going through." He turned toward me. "We gotta call the police. Like now, like this very instant."

"We can't do that."

There was an astounded silence.

"Jesus man, we're talking about your daughter!" He stared at me hollow-eyed. "You think I'll tell them about the fire. Is that it?"

I shrugged. Of course he'd tell them. Maybe not immediately, but eventually. It was his duty as one of the rich white elites, the landed gentry who ran the city. He was supposed to withhold evidence of an arson death, risk going to jail, for who... some pathetic drunk he'd only met a few days ago?

Greg frowned, looking at me. "Al, this guy sounds dangerous, maybe even psychotic. We've got to call the police. Think of Donna, for Chrissake. I mean, what are we doing here?"

"I said no cops." I ran my hand across the sharp stubble on my jaw. "You don't know this guy. If he even suspects we talked to the police, there's no telling what he'll do."

Greg shook his head in disbelief. "So what then? What's your plan?"

I stared silently out the side window.

"Al, why am I here?"

"You're here because you insisted on driving me, remember?"

"That's bullshit, Al, and you know it." He took a breath. "You're putting me in a very bad situation here. You're expecting me to walk into some kind of hostage situation with an armed psychopath. I'm sorry, but I'm not—"

"I told you, back at Chuck's. I told you it was gonna be dangerous."

"Goddamn it, Al. You didn't tell me shit."

We kept driving toward the park. For the life of me, I couldn't understand why he didn't pull over to the curb, order me out of his car, then make a beeline to the police station.

The park entrance loomed ahead.

"Just so you know, I've got about a hundred and fifty bucks on me... and the banks are closed."

"Keep it. I don't want your money."

Greg laughed, a short, mirthless laugh. "No? Then how do you plan to get your daughter back? An IOU?"

"Maybe. I don't know."

I sunk down in the leather seat and stared out the window at the passing buildings, the shuttered gas stations, the boarded-up pizza parlors and liquor stores. Only the Chinese restaurants remained open. Like cockroaches, they were indestructible.

I told myself in twenty minutes, it would all be over. Whatever happened. Only I was fooling myself. It would never be over. This part might be over, but the next part would just be beginning.

Greg shook his head and muttered, "Jesus Al." He switched on the wipers and this time he left them on. The snow was coming down hard and fast now, fat, freakishly large snowflakes the size of half dollars. The biggest ones I'd ever seen. It was like a sign or something—an omen. Probably a bad one.

I wiped the fog off the window and stared absently at the passing buildings. The city had hung lighted Santa Clauses from the light poles, the same crummy decorations I remembered from my youth. Nothing ever changed. Things just got older, shabbier, seedier.

Greg cleared his throat; when he spoke, it sounded like he was talking more to himself than to me. "This is madness. I didn't sign up for this, getting involved in all this..." He turned to face me. "I'm supposed to support you so you'll stay sober, not aid and abet a felony."

I didn't look at him. I kept my eyes on the street. I was sobering up a little, and I didn't like how it made me feel one bit. It was making me feel nervous. And a little panicky.

"I like you, Al, but goddamnit, I got to do the right thing. I have a certain standing in this town. I have obligations and a reputation."

"Sure. A reputation."

We were about to turn into the park when Greg said, "What do you say we turn around, drive over to police headquarters? I know the chief. He's a good man. If anyone can get your daughter back safe and sound, it's him. I'm just saying, me and you, we don't know what we're doing. But the chief, he's a professional. He knows this kind of thing. And I won't say a word about the fire. You have my word."

His *word*. What kind of schmuck did he take me for?

"Tell you what," I said, "why don't you just take my gun

and put a bullet in the back of my daughter's head yourself, 'cause that's what's gonna happen if we go to the cops."

Greg's eyes widened with alarm. "You have a gun?"

"What? No. I mean, not on me."

For once, I was being honest, but I don't think he believed me.

We entered the park, and Greg shook his head again. "I can't believe I'm doing this."

To be honest, I couldn't either. The park closed at dusk, which in late December came around five o'clock. There'd be bored cops cruising through from time to time looking for queers to beat up, maybe a drug dealer to work over, steal his drugs. Whatever was going to happen had to happen quickly, between patrols. We drove down a winding, snow-covered road—it was hard to tell where the road ended and the dead grass started—till we came to the little parking area near the pond, then we slowed. Hunched on a bench sat a lone figure in a snow-flecked Army surplus jacket and black wool cap. There was no sign of the Dodge. No sign of my daughter either. The Dodge must have been waiting somewhere out there in the dark.

I nodded toward the figure on the bench. "That's him. Pull over there."

"I can't believe I'm doing this..." Greg said.

I couldn't either. We came to a stop about a hundred feet from the bench; Greg kept the engine idling and the headlights on.

"You should probably kill the lights," I said.

Greg started to say something, but stopped himself. He mumbled under his breath and turned off the lights.

Barker got to his feet. It was then that I noticed the sawed-off shotgun, the stubby little barrel pointed at the ground. For the moment, Barker kept his distance.

"Wait here," I told Greg.

"Al, that guy's got a gun."

"Probably three or four."

"Al—"

I eased out of the passenger side and went around to the front of the Jaguar, trying to figure out what to do with my hands. I didn't want to hold them up like I was surrendering, because I wasn't, and I didn't want to shove them in my pockets like I was going for a weapon. When it came to my hands, there was just no good answer. I let them hang limply at my sides.

"You didn't tell me we were supposed to come packing heat," I said.

Barker glanced past me toward the Jaguar. "But I did tell you to come alone. Who the fuck's this asshole?"

"Nobody. Just my sponsor."

Barker stared at me.

"My A.A. sponsor."

"What the hell are you talking about?"

"Where's my daughter?"

Barker took a few steps toward the Jaguar and peered through the windshield at Greg. The wipers swished a layer of slush back and forth.

"Big mistake, man," Barker said. He turned back to look at me. "He fucking moves, I blow a hole through that windshield. And I would hate to do that to that Jag." He waved the barrel of the shotgun toward the bench. "Now sit over there... on your hands."

I didn't much care for his tone, but then he had the shorty, and I didn't. Anyway, the bench was exactly where I wanted to be. After I sat down—my hands firmly in my lap—Barker turned back to Greg in the Jaguar. "Okay, asshole, climb out with your hands on your head. Nice and easy."

I could literally see the color draining from Greg's face as he stared at me through the windshield. I could only shrug helplessly. Greg opened the door and put his hands on his head and slowly, and with great difficulty, got to his feet and exited the driver's side. His foot slipped on some ice and he had to grab the top of the car door to steady himself. The sudden movement surprised everyone; I thought Barker was going to blow Greg's head off right then and there.

"On the ground, face down!" Barker shouted.

Greg started to protest, but stopped when Barker racked the shotgun. Then he dropped slowly to his knees and carefully lay down on his stomach in the snow and ice. I remember thinking, *This is the last time he's going to volunteer to help out his fellow man.*

Barker squatted down next to Greg. With one hand, he pressed the barrel of the shotgun into Greg's brain stem, and with the other, he gave him a thorough frisking. He removed the wallet from Greg's back pocket, flipped it open, and studied the driver's license. Apparently, the name Schickler meant nothing to him. He left the cash in the wallet and dropped the wallet to the ground beside Greg, then he straightened and walked over to the Jaguar. "That's one sweet ride you got there, pal. What year is it, seventy-one?"

Greg lifted his head slightly. "Sixty-nine."

"Head down," Barker snapped. He walked around the Jaguar and let out a soft, appreciative whistle. "Sixty-nine? Hell of a year, Sixty-nine. Woodstock. The moon landing. Vietnam. The Manson murders." He paused. "Must've set you back a few bucks. You must be loaded, huh, fella?"

Greg hesitated. "I do all right."

"I'll bet. What are you, a lawyer or something?"

I cleared my throat from the bench. "You do know the cops patrol this park at night?"

"A pig drove through here ten minutes ago. We ought to be good for another thirty minutes, at least."

Barker's gaze shifted from Greg to me, and he said, "Take off your jacket and throw it over here."

"What?"

"Do it!"

I pulled off my jacket and tossed it to Barker. It sailed to the ground at his feet and Barker picked it up and commenced going through the pockets one by one. Finding nothing, he tossed the jacket onto the bench beside me.

"On your feet," he said.

I got up. "Why don't you make up your mind?"

"Turn around and assume the position. Hands on the back of the bench—and don't try anything smart." He glanced briefly at Greg. "That goes double for you, Rockefeller."

I did like he said. I leaned over the bench, hands resting on top of the backrest. Starting at my ankles, Barker quickly worked his way up. He'd probably been frisked enough times, he had the routine down pat. While he felt me up, my gaze drifted out across the little pond at the bottom of the hill, one clean sheet of silver ice glistening in the dark. Some Canada geese huddled noisily along the far bank. Apparently, this was as far south as they intended to go for the winter. Across the way, Christmas decorations shone brightly from one of the newer subdivisions. It all seemed so surreal, so out of sync with what was going on.

Barker finished with me and told me to sit.

"Can I put on my jacket?"

He shrugged. "Go on. We wouldn't want you catching your death."

I picked up the jacket and knocked off some of the snow and put it on.

Greg lifted his head. "Can I get up?"

Barker thought about that. "Sit down next to your buddy."

Greg got to his feet in stages. He weaved his way over to the bench and sat down beside me. He wouldn't look at me.

I cleared my throat. "Now that that's out of the way, you want to tell me where my daughter is?"

Barker cradled the shotgun in the crook of his arm while he removed a pack of Lucky Strikes and a Bic lighter from his shirt pocket and fired up a smoke. "That's some little gal you got there, Al," he said, the cigarette bobbing on his lips as he spoke. "Feisty as a pit bull. Lots of spunk."

Greg rested a hand on my arm, as if to say, *Take it easy.*
"Where is she?"

Barker blew out a cloud of smoke. "Patience, man. First, you're gonna make good on what you owe me."

I reached into my back pocket. Barker reacted by raising the shotgun. I paused, held up my other hand, and slowly pulled out my wallet. I took out the bills and held them out to him. "Here's the thousand we agreed to."

Barker pressed the barrel of the shotgun against my ribs and shoved me hard against the bench. "It's too cold and I'm too tired to be dicking around, man."

I forced myself to breathe. "Mike... buddy... I did everything you said. All of it. Loan sharks, burglary..." I cut my eyes toward Greg. "I nearly got my fool head shot off. I even asked Greg here for the money. I don't know what else I'm supposed to do. Hell, there's nothing else I *can* do." I paused to let that sink in. "Either take this grand like we agreed, or... or do what you gotta do. Only leave my daughter out of this. She's just a kid. She's got nothing to do with any of this. This here's all my fault, okay, not hers."

Barker didn't say anything, just stared at me with his cold, dead eyes as gray smoke curled around his face. I wished he would say something; his silence was creeping the hell out of me.

Finally, he nodded and turned away, then he wheeled on me. The stock of the shotgun came down fast and hard, clipping me on the side of the head—pretty much the same place he'd hit me last time. Big white stars exploded in my eyes, and I slid off the bench, crumpled to the ground, and shriveled up in pain. For a moment, I thought the son of a bitch had shot me. That's what it felt like. That's what it looked like too, with all my blood on the outside instead of inside where it belonged.

I lay in the snow, drifting in and out of consciousness, my head buzzing like a swarm of angry bees had taken up residence in my skull.

From up above me came blurred voices.

"How much for the girl?"

"Huh?"

"The girl. How much to let her go?"

"Let her go?"

"Three grand? Is that what you said?"

They faded in and out, the voices. I could hardly hear a thing above all those pissed off bees.

"Will you take a check? I can..."

"Fuck no I ain't taking no check. What do you take me for?"

It sounded like Greg was negotiating with Barker. Maybe that's all it took, one semi-lethal blow to the head. I glanced up at Greg. The bench was only about four feet away, but everything was sliding like the Tilt-A-Wheel at some strange county fair. I got my hands under me and tried to push myself up. A steel-toe boot shoved me back down. Hard.

"That's my offer... I can't get it now, but first thing in the morning, soon as the banks open. It's not a problem."

"Look... whoever the fuck you are... Al and me, we had an agreement. You and me ain't got shit. So, you wanna do what? You wanna assume his debts?"

"I can get you the cash in the morning, when the banks open. Three grand. What have you got to lose? Just give us the girl."

"You don't get it. I'm done waiting. He had twenty-four hours. Twenty eight, to be exact. No more extensions."

The bench. I had to get to that bench. I squeezed my eyes shut and blinked them open again till my vision slowly settled and cleared. Barker had moved off a good thirty yards down the road.

"Hold on!" Greg said.

Barker kept walking.

"Wait! Just a minute."

Barker stopped and turned.

"Take my car."

"What?"

"Take the Jag—as collateral. It's worth twenty grand at least. Tomorrow morning we'll meet back here, and I'll have your cash for you."

Barker started back. He walked toward Greg and stood there. "Why the hell would *you* give me three grand? I don't fucking know you."

"If that's what it takes to make sure that little girl's safe…"

They stood and looked at each other. Then Barker studied the Jaguar for a moment, probably thinking he could get a lot more than three grand out of Greg. He went over to the car and peered inside the driver's side window. Then he straightened and rested the barrel of the shotgun on his shoulder. "And the minute I take your Jag, you'll call the pigs, say it was stolen."

Greg held his hands, palms up, in front of him. "Look, mister, it's just a car. Understand I don't care what you two did, or who owes who what. Okay? All I care about is that little girl. That's it. That's all I care about. I'm gonna do whatever it takes."

"What's this kid to you?" Barker said. "Hang on, is this some kind of perverted rich guy thing? Is that what's going on here?"

Greg locked eyes with Barker. "I want to help a child, so you think I'm a pedophile?"

"I didn't say pedophile. I said pervert. Besides, I don't care what the fuck you are, long as I get my money."

There was a heavy silence. Barker studied Greg for a moment, weighing things, then he broke into a wide, shit-eating grin. "Okay, sport. You got yourself a deal. Why not? And no worries, we'll take good care of your Jag. Just like we did the girl." Barker held out his hand. "Keys."

Greg tossed the keys to Barker. Barker slipped them into his jacket pocket.

I glanced up at Greg. "How about a little help?"

Greg knelt down beside me. He got me under the armpits and lifted. "Easy does it," he said, and pulled me up onto the bench. He studied the side of my face. Judging by his look, I must have been hurt pretty bad.

"Christ, you okay, Al?"

"Sure. I didn't need all that blood, anyway."

Barker had gone down the road again and was waving a plastic orange flashlight in the air. On the far side of the pond, a pair of headlights blinked on. The lights slid sideways, then crept forward slowly through the snowfall. Barker turned off the flashlight and stuffed it into his pocket.

We watched as the vehicle crept closer. I had my arm resting along the top of the backrest. I moved down the bench a little more—though not so you would notice. I ran my hand along the back, hoping like hell it was still there.

The Dart came to a stop about thirty yards from us. I could make out the silhouette of the driver, but I couldn't see anyone else inside. The door opened and Bonnie the junkie eased out. She had on one of those short, hip-length parkas with a fake fur hood. The handle of a semi-automatic showed above her jeans. You couldn't miss it if you tried.

I wiped some of the blood and snow out of my eyes with my jacket sleeve. "Where's my daughter?" I said.

They ignored me. Bonnie studied the scene and turned to Barker. "Did you get it, babe?"

"We're taking the Jag."

A flicker of confusion crossed her face. "Jag? What are you talking about?"

Barker tossed away his cigarette, but didn't say anything.

"I don't understand," she said. "Did you get it or not?"

"We're taking the car."

She glanced around and slowly shook her head, like she'd been given some kind of unfathomable riddle to puzzle out. "*That* wasn't the plan," she cried. "You can't just change the plan without talking to me!"

"I know it wasn't the plan, but it's the plan now. Go get the girl."

"Don't tell me what to do!"

They glared at each other for a moment, then the girlfriend backed down. She narrowed her eyes and folded her arms over the parka, then she went back to the Dodge and opened the back door. A second later, I saw my daughter's head pop up. Bonnie pulled her out of the back seat and dragged her from the vehicle. My daughter's mouth was gagged with some kind of handkerchief and her eyes were wide and wet with terror. She was still wearing the black dress she had worn to Frank's wake—but no coat. They had bound her hands behind her with clothesline.

Those eyes found me the same moment I found my semi-automatic duct taped to the back of the bench.

Bonnie shoved my daughter toward the bench and Donna stumbled and fell to the ground. Her head struck the edge of the wooden seat.

Something caught fire inside me. I felt all the air around my head close in. I gave the pistol a hard tug and the duct tape gave way. My finger found the trigger and I squeezed for all I was worth. The pistol boomed and kicked like an angry mule. Barker wore this surprised look, a look I hadn't seen since Korea a half second after some poor sumbitch stepped on a landmine. Before he could get the shotgun up, I put another slug in him, slightly left of center. He stumbled back, one, two steps. He tried, but he couldn't get the barrel up. His eyes rolled back in his head and he seemed to give up. He let go of the shotgun and sat down spread legged in the snow.

Bonnie let loose a good, healthy shriek and ran to his side. It was touching in a way. True junkie love. She must have forgotten all about the pistol in her jeans. Anyway, she never even went for it. It only took one in the guts to drop her. She let out a small cry and flopped over onto Barker's lap.

Then it got real quiet. Gunsmoke hung on the night air like a fine mist.

Barker sat in a puddle of red slush, fighting for air. Watching him lying there struggling to breathe reminded me of this little old gray squirrel I shot with a .22 when I was nine years old. The first real thing I ever killed. I remember standing over him at the time, mesmerized, watching as the little squirrel breaths got slower and slower and finally ceased altogether. The squirrel's black, terrified eyes on me, the instrument of its death. It took less than a minute, then it was still. No more suffering. No more squirrel troubles.

Barker didn't last much longer.

I wiped some more blood from my eyes, then I kicked away the shotgun. I lost my balance and fell to one knee. Whatever I had was a lot worse than a concussion—though I wasn't complaining too much. I was still a lot better off than Barker and his girl.

I shoved the pistol into my waistband and turned to my daughter. Blood trickled from a bruised cut above her right eye. Donna and Greg stood staring at me, sharing a look of shock and disbelief.

"Jesus, Al!" Greg said. "You didn't have to do that! I was gonna give them the money!"

I glared angrily at Greg. Up till now, I hadn't had any ill feelings toward him. But now he was acting like I was the bad guy.

Fine. Whatever. That would make only make easier what I had to do.

"What—you feel sorry for them?" I cried. "That sumbitch killed my son! He kidnapped my daughter! God only knows what he did to her."

Greg shook his head. There it was again, that old, familiar look of disgust mixed with disappointment. I may as well have been talking to my mother.

I went to remove the gag from Donna's mouth, but she backed away when I approached her, like she thought I might turn the pistol on her next.

"Did they hurt you, honey?" I said. "Tell me. What did they do to you?"

She must have been in shock. I don't think she could talk. Greg took off his leather jacket and wrapped it around her shoulders. She let him. He helped her over to the bench and got her to sit down. Then he went over and squatted down beside Barker and the girl. He started checking the girl's pulse.

"She's still breathing. We've got to get her to the hospital."

I looked at my daughter. A long string of snot dripped from one of her nostrils. She didn't seem to notice that or anything else. "I'm sorry you had to see that, honey. I…"

Greg got to his feet. He walked over to his Jaguar and started going through the vehicle. I couldn't figure out what he was doing. He came back with a pocketknife and began cutting the clothesline from my daughter's wrists. He removed the gag. He asked her if she was okay, but she didn't respond to him either. He asked her if she'd like to go sit in his car.

Nothing.

He helped her to the car anyway and put her in the back seat so she wouldn't have to look at the pile of dead people.

The snow fell harder now. Not like a blizzard though, because the wind had died down and everything had gotten winter-night quiet. I knew the cops would be along any minute now. I went over to where Barker and the girl lay. Barker was sitting there, same as he'd fallen, only now he had a dead girl in his lap. I picked up the shotgun. I cracked open the barrels. Two 12-gauge shells were locked and loaded.

I guess I'd known all along, the way it would have to go down. At least from the moment I'd fled Russ' house. Knew the only way to get my daughter back was Greg's Jaguar. And the only way to get Greg and his Jag to the park was to let him in on him everything—the kidnapping and everything that led up to it. And that once I'd gotten rid of Barker—for there was no way I was going to let that bastard walk away from this—Greg would be the only one left who could tie me to my son's death. And to Barker and his girl.

The only one left who's testimony could send me to the chair.

The easy part was over. Shooting Barker and his girlfriend, that had been as simple as stepping on a bug. Easier, because unlike a bug, they deserved it.

Greg leaned against the hood of his car and folded his arms across his chest. His jaw was as rigid as a horseshoe.

"Okay, Al, so now what?"

I listened for sirens, but there weren't any I could hear. A few geese honked across the pond. Somewhere, far across town, a train whistled long and lonesome. I'd been hearing that same train my whole life. It used to be a comfort.

I studied Barker and the girl and put the scene together in my head. There was a good chance the cops would make the scene for a drug deal gone wrong. A rich junky meeting two low-life drug dealers in the park at night. If we started now, if we cut through the park and came out on the other end, and found a phone booth where we could call a cab... There was a chance we could make it back to my car.

Then what?

Alaska maybe. Florida.

I'd forgotten all about the dope. Chances were Barker had drugs on him somewhere, him or the girl, but I had to be sure. I squatted down next to Barker, and I took out the bag I'd bought off the bikers and stuffed it into his jacket pocket.

I could feel Greg's eyes on me, but he kept silent. Probably nothing I could do would surprise him now. I got to my feet. I had felt only blind rage when I shot Barker and the girl. But now all that remained was that sick feeling I had after shooting Russ and Sandy. And maybe a couple of times in Korea.

I racked the shotgun. "Move away from the car."

Greg had his arms crossed; he gave me a look of infinite disgust that seemed to say he was done playing around. "What are you gonna do, Al?" he said. "You gonna shoot me?"

I glanced toward the back seat. I couldn't see anything. I couldn't see if Donna was watching. Maybe she was. I hoped not. Maybe she was in shock and didn't know what the hell was going on. I sure hoped so.

Near the entrance to the park, red and blue lights spun and flashed as a patrol car entered the park. Someone must have reported the shots after all. I stared hard at the snow beneath my feet, trying to force my thoughts to get in line. There were all these footprints in the snow. Mine and Donna's and Greg's and Barker's and Barker's girl's. It was coming down hard, but not hard enough to hide all those sets of prints. Not by the time that patrolman got here. Even our rube cops couldn't help but notice there were more than three people out here. They'd see our prints trekking off across the park like a trail of breadcrumbs.

And how was I going to get Donna across the park? Carry her? I could barely stand up myself.

And I still had Greg to deal with. I gave him a shove with the barrel of the shotgun. "Over by the bench," I said.

He didn't move. "Al, listen to me. It's over... Your daughter's safe. Isn't that what you wanted? Isn't that what's important? Let's stop all this. What's the point of going on?" He paused. "Buddy, what are we doing here?"

The back door of the Jaguar opened and Donna got out. She stood with her hand on the door. She didn't say anything.

Greg gave me a look of profound pity. "For Chrissake, Al, think of your daughter. Take my car and leave Donna with me. I'll see she gets home to her mother."

Her mother. I didn't even want to think about that.

I grabbed Greg by his jacket and pulled him off the car. I dragged him a few feet and gave him a shove. He stumbled and fell on his ass in the snow. I kept the barrel on him.

I said, "Donna, get back in the car."

Greg said, "Al, for Chrissake, think about what you're doing! Hasn't she been through enough already?"

"Shut your goddamn mouth! I've heard enough outta you!"

Greg's tone softened. "Please Al. Just take my car and go."

Sure, I could take the Jaguar. And I wouldn't get five miles before a deputy or a state trooper pulled me over.

"Al, I wanna go home," Donna said. Her voice sounded very far away.

I locked eyes with Greg. "Donna, get back in the car!"

She wasn't listening. I was going to have to force her back into the car. No way could I subject her to this, too. That was too much.

Greg got to his feet. He came toward me, slowly, his hand held out in front of him, his voice firm, grave. "Alright Al, that's enough of this. Give me the gun."

He'd either lost his mind or he wasn't taking me seriously. I took a step back. "Back off, Greg!"

He didn't. "Al, this is crazy. You're not a bad guy. Those two, okay, they deserved it. But you're not a killer. You didn't mean for anything to happen to your son."

My daughter turned to me, panic flaring in her eyes. "What'd he say about Frank? Al? What's he talking about?"

The lousy, big-mouthed bastard! That rotten son of a bitch! He had to open his goddamn trap... He had to ruin everything. The only thing that wasn't ruined.

"What's he mean? Al, what's he mean about Frank?"

"Don't pay any attention to him, honey." I turned back to Greg. "You've got a big mouth, you know that, mister?"

Greg had this mortified look on his face, like he'd just realized he'd said something unforgivable. But did that stop him? Hell no. There was only one way to stop him.

He came on determinedly, his hand out. "The gun, Al."

I crooked my finger on the trigger. "You could have prevented all this with a couple thousand bucks. But no, you had to stick to your principles. Well, this is where your goddamn principles get you."

"Al, for your daughter's sake..."

The cruiser's spotlight washed over the trunks and bare branches. The red and blue lights flashed on the snow. Everything seemed to glow.

And the snow kept falling like nothing was happening.

"Why?" I cried. "Why couldn't you keep your goddamn mouth shut?"

Something slammed into me from behind. It felt like being rammed by a bull.

It happened again, knocking me to my knees. The sounds floated out over the park and skipped across the frozen pond. There were screams, sirens. I couldn't connect any of it. There was too much coming too fast.

The snow on the ground before me was speckled red. As I slumped to the ground, I saw Bonnie sitting up, hands gripping the pistol. She slowly lowered the barrel and looked at me. Then her eyes went blank.

I remember thinking, this ain't so bad. I've been through worse. A lot worse. Hell, they make a big deal out of it. This ain't nothing.

A siren wound down. There were people moving around, doing things, and underwater sounds, but none of it seemed to have anything to do with me.

You know you've reached the end when there's nothing there. You're not there. Just nothingness. And none of it matters. Whether you live or die.

Then everything fades. Everything gets quiet.

It's been that way ever since.

CHRIS ORLET is the author of two novels, *A Taste of Shotgun* (All Due Respect) and *In the Pines* (New Pulp Press) and a contributor to *Dirty Boulevard: Stories based on the Songs of Lou Reed* (Down & Out Books). He lives in Saint Louis, Missouri.

On the following pages are a few
more great titles from the
Down & Out Books publishing family.

For a complete list of books and to
sign up for our newsletter,
go to DownAndOutBooks.com.

The Comeback
A Duffy Mystery
Tom Schreck

Down & Out Books
August 2023
978-1-64396-326-6

After almost a decade, our social-working, pro-boxing, Schlitz-drinking, basset hound-loving, bleeding heart tough guy, Duffy, has no idea what he's in for. His world literally blows up with a new gig, a career shift, another hound and, though he's still spending most of the time in AJ's, now it is from the other side of the bar.

On the trail to get even for a friend, he's up against the Chicago Mob, the city's toughest street gang and a crooked doctor preying on the addicted.

Waking Up the Devil
Chris Miller

Down & Out Books
August 2023
978-1-64396-325-9

A master killer is forced back into the business, and it's personal. Cade Samson has less than a day to take out his old partner before his former crime boss murders his brother. The problem is, the Feds are all over it.

Get ready for a pedal to the metal splatterfest of crime and vengeance.

"Chris Miller is one of the best kept secrets in crime fiction. But he won't be a secret anymore once readers get ahold of this masterful new offering." —Andy Rausch, author of *Hell To Pay*

Loud Water
Robby Henson

Down & Out Books
August 2023
978-1-64396-327-3

Eight years into a 15-year sentence, Crit Poppwell finally discovered something he was good at, besides destroying his family and abusing drugs. He found art. The solitary act of drawing, painting and creating brings a calmness to his chaos.

Crit returns to his hometown where his brother is the reigning crystal meth kingpin and his ex-wife wants him dead. Can Crit flush the past from his blood and bones? Or die trying?

"A brilliant noir debut with a bittersweet ending."
—Jim Winter, author of the Holland Bay series

Killin' Time in San Diego
Bouchercon Anthology 2023
Holly West, Editor

Down & Out Books
August 2023
978-1-64396-328-0

Welcome to San Diego, where the perpetual sunshine blurs the line between good and evil, and sin and redemption are two sides of the same golden coin.

Killin' Time in San Diego is a gripping anthology featuring twenty of today's best crime and mystery writers and published in conjunction with Bouchercon 2023.

From the haunted hallways of the Hotel del Coronado to the tranquil gardens of Balboa Park, from the opulent estates of La Jolla to the bustling Gaslamp Quarter, *Killin' Time in San Diego* is your ticket to the hidden side of "America's Finest City."

www.ingramcontent.com/pod-product-compliance
Lightning Source LLC
Chambersburg PA
CBHW031150020426
42333CB00013B/594